Oxford Progressi
General Edit

The Thimble a

MORETON HALL
FICTION LIBRARY

The *Oxford* ....
ra............................ English. It includes some of the
favourite stories of young readers, and also modern fiction. The
.... made at a 1400 word
.... word level. *Grade 2* at a 2100 word
.... word level and *Grade 4* which consists of
.... Structural, as well as lexical controls are
applied ....

.... the mood and style of the original stories
have been retained. Where this requires departure from the
grading scheme, glosses and notes are given.

All the books in the series are attractively illustrated. Each
book also has a short section containing questions and suggested
activities for students.

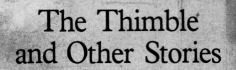

The Thimble
and Other Stories

D.H. Lawrence

Hong Kong
OXFORD UNIVERSITY PRESS
Oxford Singapore Tokyo
1984

Oxford University Press

Oxford London New York Toronto
Kuala Lumpur Singapore Hong Kong Tokyo
Delhi Bombay Calcutta Madras Karachi
Nairobi Dar es Salaam Cape Town
Melbourne Auckland
and associated companies in
Beirut Berlin Ibadan Mexico City Nicosia

© *Oxford University Press 1984*
This edition first published 1984

OXFORD is a trade mark of Oxford University Press

Retold by Jack C. Richards
Illustrated by Penelope Wurr
Simplified according to the language grading scheme
especially compiled by D.H. Howe

ISBN 0 19 581363 4

Printed by New Kwok Hing Printing Press Co Ltd.
3/F 44 Lee Chung St., Hong Kong.
Published by Oxford University Press,
Warwick House, Quarry Bay, Hong Kong.

Contents

D.H. Lawrence was born in 1885 in England. He was the son of a miner and became a schoolmaster before turning to writing as a profession. Although he lived for many years in Italy, Australia and New Mexico, the years spent in England during the First World War provide the background for many of his Short Stories. *The Thimble,* included in this collection of stories, is a typical example.

He died in 1930.

I

The Thimble

Married but alone

She had not seen her husband for ten months, not since the two weeks they had spent together for their honeymoon before he went off to the war in France. The excitement of the war had made them almost like brother and sister. But now all that was shut off from her mind. Since then, since the honeymoon,   *5* she had lived and died and come to life again. She had loved him then.

'If you want to love your husband,' she had told her friends proudly, 'you should see him in his soldier's uniform.' And she had really loved him. He was so handsome in uniform; well   *10* built, yet with a sort of coldness that suited the colour of his uniform perfectly.

Before, when he was a young lawyer with nothing to do, she had not thought much of him, and she had never come to the point of marrying him. For one thing, neither of them had   *15* enough money.

Then came the great shock of the war. He came to her in a new light, as a lieutenant. And she had been deeply struck by his perfect, calm manliness, now that he was a soldier. He seemed to have gained a fascinating importance that made her   *20* seem quite unimportant. It was he who was dignified and she who was insignificant.

So she married him and had known the bewildering* experience of their fortnight's honeymoon, before he left her for the war.   *25*

And she had never got over the bewilderment. She had, since then never thought at all. She seemed to have rushed on in a storm of activity. There was a home to make, and no money to make it with. So, with the swift, business-like mind of

bewildering, confusing; puzzling.

I

a startled woman, she had found a small flat in Mayfair*, had attended sales and bought suitable furniture, had made the place complete and perfect. She was satisfied. It was small and insignificant, but it was complete.

5 Then she had had a certain amount of war-work to do, and she had kept up all her social activities. She had not had a moment which was not urgently occupied.

All the while came his letters from France, and she was writing her replies. They both sent a good deal of news to each 10 other. They both expressed their mutual passion.

Then suddenly, in the middle of all this activity, she fell ill with pneumonia and everything collapsed. And while she was ill, he was wounded, his jaw smashed and his face cut up by the bursting of a shell. So they were both recovering.

15 Now they were both better, and she was waiting to see him. She had gone to her parents' home in Scotland when she was ill and there she had thought. For she was a woman who was always trying to understand things around her, always trying to make a complete thing of her own life.

Changes

20 Her illness lay between her and her previous life like a dark night; like a great separation. She looked back; she remembered all she had done, and she was puzzled. But she had no key to the puzzle. Suddenly she realized that she knew nothing of this man she had married. He knew nothing of her. 25 What she knew of him was the memory of him, the visual image. She could *see* him, the whole of him, in her mind's eye but he was an impression, only a vivid* impression.

What was he, himself, she asked herself? The very thought startled her. It was like looking through a frightening darkness. 30 All that she knew of him was her own personal impression. But there was a *man*, another being, somewhere in the darkness which she was frightened to enter.

*Mayfair, a fashionable district in the West End of London. *vivid, very clear.

She could hardly bare to think of him as she knew him before. She hated thinking back to the memory of the days of her honeymoon. It was something false. It was something which had only to do with herself. The man himself was something different, something she was afraid of. 5

Nervously she twisted her long white fingers. She was a beautiful woman, tall and rather thin, with swinging limbs; one for whom the modern fashions were perfect. Her skin was pure and clear like a Christmas rose. Her hair was fair and heavy. She had large, slow eyes, that sometimes looked blue 10 and open, almost childlike, sometimes greenish and deep in thought, and sometimes grey and pathetic.

Now she sat in her own room in the flat in Mayfair, and he was coming to see her. She was well again: just well enough to see him. But she was tired as she sat in the chair while the maid 15 arranged her heavy, fair hair.

She knew she was beautiful. She knew people expected her to look like an image of modern beauty. And it pleased her; it made her soul rather hard and proud: but also, it bored her.

She wanted to have her hair combed high as was the fashion. 20 She lifted her eyes to look. They were slow, greenish, and cold like the sea at this moment because she was puzzled. She was trying to understand and to adjust herself. She never thought to expect anything of the other person; she was utterly independent. 25

'No,' she said to her maid, in her slow, intense voice. 'Don't let it swell out over the ears, lift it straight up, then twist it under . . . like that . . . so it goes clean from the side of the face. Do you see?'

'Yes my lady.' 30

She was getting dressed now to see her husband. She felt heavy and cold, yet inside she was trembling. It was not the man that she knew who frightened her. It was the unknown man. What was he? Her dark unknown soul trembled.

Anyway, he would be different. She gave a startled jump. 35 The vision she remembered of him: good-looking, clean, with a dark tan, attractive, understanding. This image she must try

3

to forget. They said his face was rather horribly cut up. She
shivered. How she hated the thought of his physical injuries.
Her fingers trembled. She rose to go downstairs.

So in her fashionable but inexpensive black silk dress,
wearing her jewels, she went downstairs. She knew how to   5
walk, how to hold her body, how to create the right impression.

Entering the small drawing-room, she lifted her eyes slowly
and looked at herself: a tall woman in black, with fair hair,
and with slow, greenish, cold eyes looking into the mirror. She
turned away with a cold look of satisfaction. She was aware also   10
of the signs of weariness and illness and age, in her face. She
was twenty-seven years old.

Waiting

So she sat on the little sofa by the fire. She liked the room she
had made, with its light-brown walls, its deep-brown carpet,
and the furniture covered in a red cloth she had bought at a   15
sale. She looked at her own large feet, upon the rose-red
Persian rug.

Then, nervously, yet quite calmly, she sat still to wait. It was
one of the moments of deepest suffering and suspense which
she had ever known. She did not want to think of his physical   20
injuries. She would wait and see what her reaction was to the
man, the unknown stranger, who was coming to take her soul!
She could not bear it. Her face turned pale. She began to lose
consciousness.

Then something whispered in her: 'If I am like this, I shall   25
not be able to respond to him. I will only see the surface of
him.' Nervously she pressed her hands down onto the sofa at
her side. She pressed hard upon the worn covering.

Her hands began to move slowly backwards and forwards on
the sofa bed, slowly, as if the feeling of the cloth on her fingers   30
gave her some comfort.

She was unaware of what she was doing. She was always so
calm, so self-contained. She was too intelligent to show any
outward signs of embarrassment. But now she sat there,

rubbing her hands back and forth, back and forth, pleading, hoping for an answer.

Her right hand came to the end of the sofa and pressed a little into the crack, the meeting between the arm and the sofa
5 bed. Her long white fingers pressed into the crack, pressed further and further into the tight opening, while her mind was elsewhere, and the firelight flickered on the yellow flowers that stood in a jar on the window.

The thimble

Then working slowly, her fingers pressed deeper and deeper
10 into the sofa, pressed and worked their way to the bottom. It was the bottom. They were there. They made sure. Then they touched a little object. The woman's mind awoke. What was it? She touched again. It was something hard and rough. Her fingers began to turn it round. It had a thin edge like a ring,
15 but it was not a ring. Her fingers worked again. What was this little hard object?

Her fingers moved it slowly up into the light. It was coming. There was success. The woman's heart relaxed from its tension. Her long white fingers brought out the little object.
20 It was a thimble. It was old and rather heavy, made of gold, with little diamonds and rubies set round the base. Perhaps it was not gold, and perhaps the stones were not real?

She put it on her sewing finger. The stones sparkled in the firelight. She was pleased. It was a common, ugly thing. It was
25 large too, big enough for her. It must have been some woman's sewing thimble. But it was heavy. It would make one's hand ache.

She began to rub the gold with her handkerchief. There was an initial, Z, and someone's monogram*, and a date: 15 Oct.
30 1801. She was very pleased, thinking of an old romance. What did Z stand for? Was he an earl? Who would give the gift of a gold thimble set with jewels, in the year 1801? Perhaps it was a

monogram, two or more letters woven together; usually the initials of someone's name.

man who had come home from the wars?

Just then the maid opened the door and saw her mistress sitting in the soft light of the winter day, polishing something with her handkerchief.

'Mr Hepburn has come, my lady.' 5

'Has he?' answered the woman with a start.

She collected herself and rose. Her husband was coming through the doorway, past the maid. He came without his hat or gloves, like someone who belonged in the house . . . an inmate. He was an inmate of the house. 10

'How do you do,' she said calmly, but helplessly. And she held out her hand.

'How are *you*?' he replied in a muffled voice.

'All right now, thanks,' and she sat down again, her heart beating violently. She had not yet looked at his face. The 15 muffled voice terrified her so much.

Without thinking, she put the thimble on her middle finger, and continued to rub it with her handkerchief. The man sat in silence opposite, in an armchair. She was aware of his brown trousers and his heavy shoes. But she was concentrating on 20 polishing the thimble. Her mind was in a trance; as if she were on the point of waking up for the first time in her life.

A difficult meeting

'What are you doing? What have you got?' asked the mumbling, muffled voice. A pain went through her. She looked up at the mouth that produced the sound. It was 25 broken in, the bottom teeth all gone, the side of the chin battered small, while a deep, horrible scar ran right into the middle of the cheek. But the mouth was the worst. Half the lip was cut away.

'It is a little hidden treasure,' answered the cold-sounding 30 voice. And she held out the thimble.

He reached to take it. His hand was white, and it trembled. His nerves were broken. He took the thimble between his fingers and turning it, he looked at it closely.

7

She sat frozen, as if his injuries were photographed upon her mind. All she could see was his disfigurement*: the dreadful, broken mouth that was not a mouth, which mumbled when talking to her. It was not real. She felt like a person trapped in

5 a horrible dream who was trying to wake up so that it would go away.

'Why do you call it a hidden treasure?' he mumbled. She could not understand him.

She felt his moment's hesitation before he tried again, and a

10 hot pain pierced through her. 'Hidden treasure, you said,' he repeated, struggling to speak clearly.

'I found it,' she said. Her voice was clear but cold. 'I found it just before you came in.'

There was a silence between them. It seemed to go on

15 forever. With a strange struggle, she broke into conversation with him.

'I found it here, in the sofa,' she said, and she lifted her eyes to him for the first time.

His forehead was white, and his hair brushed smooth, like a

20 sick man's. And his eyes were like the eyes of a child that had been ill, blue and distant, as if they only saw from a long way off. He looked almost like a child that belonged more to death than to life. She lowered her eyelids, and for a second she sat like a statue with closed eyes. Then she opened her eyes. She

25 was awake. She looked at him. His eyes were still abstract and without answer.

'Did you really?' he asked. 'Why, how did it come there?'

It was the same voice, the same man as before. Only the voice was different, the words all mumbled as if his speech

30 itself was disintegrating.

Her heart shrank. Yet once more she lifted her eyes and looked at him. His eyes were flickering, looking at the things around him.

'I suppose it got pushed down by accident,' she said,

35 answering from her mechanical mind.

*disfigurement, spoilt appearance usually caused by some injury or accident.

8

But her eyes were watching him as if he were dead.

'How did it happen?' she said, and her voice was changed, sad and filled with pity. He knew what she meant.

'Well you see I was knocked out, and that was all I knew for three days. But it seems it was a shell, fired by one of our own men, and it hit me because it had a fault in it.'

Her face was very still as she watched.

'And how did you feel when you woke up?'

'I felt very bad, as you can imagine; there was a crack on my skull as well as on my jaw.'

'Did you think you were going to die?'

There was a long pause, while the man laughed self-consciously. But he laughed only with the upper part of his face. The injured part did not move. And though the eyes seemed to laugh, just like before, underneath them was a black challenging darkness. Then came the mumbling speech.

'Yes, I lay and looked at death.'

The darkness of his eyes was now watching her. She almost wanted to say, 'And why didn't you die?' But instead she looked helplessly at him.

'I couldn't, while you were alive,' he said.

'What?'

'Die.'

She seemed to pass away into unconsciousness. Then when she woke up she said, as if in protest, 'What difference should *I* make to you! You can't live off me.'

He was watching her with dull, sightless eyes. There was a long silence. She was thinking, it was not her consciousness of him that had kept *her* alive. It was her own will.

'What did you hope for, from me?' she asked.

His eyes darkened. His face seemed very white. He really looked like a dead man as he sat silent and with open, sightless eyes. He balanced the thimble between his trembling fingers. Watching him, a darkness seemed to come over her. She could not see. He was only a presence near her in the dark.

'Both of us are helpless,' she said into the silence.

'Helpless for what?' answered his mumbling voice.

'To live,' she said. 'We are helpless to live.'

They seemed to be talking to each other's souls. Their eyes and minds were sightless.

'We are helpless to live,' he repeated.

5 'Yes,' she said.

There was still a silence.

'I know,' he said. 'We are helpless to live. I knew that when I came round*.'

'I am as helpless as you are,' she said.

10 'Yes, I know that. You're as helpless as I am.'

'Well then,' she said.

'Well then, we are helpless. We are as helpless as babies,' he said.

There was a long pause. Then she laughed brokenly.

15 'I don't know,' she said. 'A helpless baby can't know whether it likes being a helpless baby.'

Hope

'That's just the same. But I feel *hope*. Don't you?'

Again there was an unwilling pause on her part.

'Hope of what?'

20 'If I am a helpless baby now, then I shall grow into a man.'

She gave a slightly amused laugh.

'And I ought to hope that I shall grow into a woman,' she said.

'Yes of course.'

25 'Then what am I now?' she asked humorously.

'Now you're a helpless baby, as you said.'

It annoyed her a little. But she knew it was true.

'And what was I before . . . when I married you?' she asked.

'Why, I don't know what you were like then. That was

30 before my accident. It's all gone. Don't you see?'

'I see.'

There was a pause. She became aware of the room around

*came round, regained consciousness.

her and of the fire burning low and red.

'And what are we doing together?' she said.

'We're going to love each other,' he said.

'Didn't we love each other before,' she asked challengingly.

'No we couldn't. We weren't born.'   5

'Neither were we dead,' she answered.

'Are we dead now?' he asked in fear.

'Yes we are.'

There was a deadly silence. It was so true.

'Then we must be born again,' he said.   10

'Must we?' said her deliberate voice.

'Yes we must, otherwise . . .' He did not finish.

'And do you think we've got the power to come to life again, now we're dead?' she asked.

'I think we have,' he said.   15

There was a long pause.

'It takes time,' he said.

The pain of his statement made her jerk up with a little laugh. At the same time her face contracted and she said in a loud voice, as if her soul were being torn from her, 'Am I going   20
to love you?'

Again he stretched forward and touched her hand with the tips of his fingers. Then after a while he noticed that the thimble was stuck on his little finger. In the same instant she also looked at it.   25

'I want to throw it away,' he said.

Again she gave a little jerk of laughter.

He rose, went to the window, and opened it. Then, suddenly with a strong movement of the arm and shoulder, he threw the thimble out into the street. It bounced on the pavement   30
opposite. Then a taxi went by, and he could not see it anymore.

2
Prelude

In the kitchen of a small farm, a little woman sat cutting bread and butter. Her cheeks glowed from the red of the fire. She skillfully spread the softened butter and cut off slices from the floury loaf in her lap. The wind outside blew against the door.
5 The grey-haired woman looked up, rose and went to look out. The sky was heavy and grey. She turned away, took a cloth from the table and lifted the bread out of the oven. Afterwards she laid the table for five.

She hurried about, putting milk and other things on the
10 table, lifting the potatoes from the fire, peeping* through the window anxiously. There was a click of the gate. She ran to the window, then filled the teapot with hot water. There was the sound of boots outside the door, then the door opened and a strong, bearded* man entered. He was a man who looked as if
15 he had worked hard all his life. It was her husband.

The family

'Hello,' he said loudly and cheerfully. 'Am I the first? Aren't any of the boys back yet? Fred will be here in a minute.'

'I wish they would come,' said the wife, 'or else it will rain before they get here.'

20 'Yes, it won't be long before it does rain,' he said, and he sat down heavily in his chair, looking at his wife as she knelt and took a large jar of cooked apples from the oven.

'Well dear,' he said, with a pleasant, comfortable little smile. 'It's nearly Christmas again. Christmas comes and goes,
25 doesn't it!'

'Yes,' she said, 'it does, but we always seem to be just as poor. This year was especially disappointing.'

---

peeping, taking a quick look. *bearded*, having hair on the lower part of the face.

'It seems so,' he said, looking a little sad for a moment. 'This year we have certainly had some very bad luck.'

'Yes, poor Fred has hardly made any money at all this year,' she added, 'nor have the two boys working in the mine*.'

'Well, what can I do? If I hadn't lost my last crop of hay, and   *5* those two cows . . .'

'If . . . I wonder what is going to happen to Fred? He has worked on the farm for you for years now, and still he has nothing. When you were his age, when you were twenty-five, you were married and had two children. How can he ask   *10* anybody to marry him?'

'Don't you worry about him, dear. He's fairly happy. Besides, we may have a good year next year.'

'So you say.'

'Don't worry about things. It's true, things haven't gone as   *15* we hoped they would. I never thought I would see you having to work so hard, but really, we have been quite comfortable, haven't we?'

'Well, I never thought my oldest son would be a farm labourer when he was twenty-five, and the other two working   *20* in the coal-mine.'

Just then there was a sound outside and the eldest son came in. He was covered in mud. He took off his wet coat, and stood in front of the fire with his hands spread out to warm them. He smiled at his mother as she moved about in the kitchen and   *25* said, 'You do look warm and cozy there Mother, in your new apron, getting tea ready and watching the weather. Oh there are the boys.'

She gave a little laugh and poured out the tea. The boys came in from the mine, wet and dirty, with clean streaks down   *30* their faces where the rain had run. They changed their clothes and sat at the table. The elder was a big, heavy fellow with a long nose and chin. The younger, Arthur, was a handsome boy with dark hair and deep eyes. When he talked and laughed the red of his lips and the whiteness of his teeth and eyeballs stood   *35*

---

*mine, a hole dug to get coal or metal from the ground.

out in startling contrast to the surrounding black.

'Mother, I'm glad to see you,' he said, looking at her affectionately*.

She took a bite of bread and butter and looked up with a
5   smile.

'Well,' said Henry, 'it's Christmas Eve. The fire ought to burn its brightest.'

'Yes. What are we going to do, Mother? Are we going to have a party?'

10   'Yes, if you want one.'

'A party?' laughed the father. 'Who would come?'

'We might ask somebody. We could ask Nellie Wycherley. She used to come here when she was a young girl. And David Garton.'

15   'I doubt if Nellie will want to come here nowadays,' said the father. 'I saw her driving in her new car on Sunday morning, with another young woman. She stopped and asked me if we had any holly* growing on our land, to decorate her house for Christmas. I said we hadn't.'

20   Fred looked up from the book he was reading. He had dark-brown eyes, something like his mother's, and they always drew attention when he turned them on anyone.

'There is a holly tree covered in berries, in the woods,' he said.

25   'Well,' answered Henry, 'if she is so proud that she doesn't want to visit us anymore, then I'm not going to cut down holly for her. If she came to the house and asked, I wouldn't mind. But when she sits in her car and looks down on you and asks, "Do you happen to have any holly with berries? Mr Preston my
30   servant, can't find any to decorate the house, and I have some people coming down from town." Then I tell her that we haven't got any, and we want it even more than her because nobody is coming to visit us, neither from the town nor the country, and we are likely to forget it's Christmas if we don't
35   have anybody or anything to remind us of it.'

---

*affectionately, with love. *holly, evergreen bush with prickly leaves and red berries.

'What did she say?' asked the mother.

'She said she was sorry to have bothered us. Then she and her friend started laughing. Then Nellie asked me if we were going to do a Christmas play this year.'

In that part of the country people often visited neighbours at   5
Christmas and performed a short Christmas play. Fred and his brothers were famous in the neighbourhood for a little play they used to perform.

'I said we weren't doing it this year.'

'Nellie and her friends will have nobody to laugh at tonight,'   10
said Arthur.

A Christmas play

'Well, why don't we go!' exclaimed Henry. 'Hey!' he suddenly shouted to Fred who was reading and taking no notice. 'Hey, we're going to the Wycherleys' house tonight.'

'Who is?' asked the elder brother, a little surprised.   15

'You and me and Arthur. I'll play the part of Beelzebub, the Devil.'

He made a strange face, so that everyone laughed.

'Go,' said his father, 'you'll make a fortune!'

'What,' he replied, 'by making a fool of myself? What will   20
you be Arthur?'

'I don't care,' was the answer. 'We can put some red paint and some charcoal from the fire on our faces. Shall we go, Fred?'

'I don't know.'   25

'Why, I would like to see her with all her fine friends from the town. We could take her some holly and leave it at the back of the house.'

'All right then.'

After they had finished their tea, Fred took a lamp and went   30
into the woods to cut some of the holly. When he got back he found his brothers laughing loudly in front of the mirror. They were covered with red and black and had put on huge moustaches so that they were entirely unrecognizable.

Fred washed and got ready. He refused to paint his face, so he wrapped himself in a rug and tied a white cloth around his head to make himself look like an Arab. He looked at himself and was pleased with the result. Then he took an old sword
5 from the wall and held it in one hand.

'Well,' he said, 'that doesn't look too bad, does it?'

'Oh that's great,' said his mother, as he entered the kitchen. His dark eyes glowed with pleasure to hear her say it. He seemed somewhat excited. His dark skin shone rich and warm
10 under the white cloth. His eyes glittered like a true Arab. The way he had folded the rug around him made him look like a true warrior.

They set out to cross the fields to their neighbours, the Wycherleys. A little snow was falling. The ground was wet and
15 the night was very dark. But they knew the way well and were soon at the gate leading up to the yard of the house. The dog began to bark loudly, but they called to him, 'Trip, Trip,' and knowing their voices, he became quiet.

Henry gave a loud knock on the door and called out loudly,
20 'Here comes Beelzebub. Here comes Beelzebub!'

A big farm girl came to the door. 'Who is it?' she asked.

'Beelzebub. You know him well,' was the answer.

'I'll ask Miss Ellen if she wants to see you.'

Henry smiled at the maid, and stepped into the house to
25 wait. The girl ran away and soon there was laughing and bright talk of women's voices drawing nearer to the kitchen.

'Tell them to come into the kitchen,' said a voice.

The three boys walked into the kitchen and looked around the huge room. They could only see Betty, seated near to them
30 on a chair. Her father was in a corner in a big armchair, looking black and sour faced.

There were two women sitting in another dark corner.

'Well,' said Beelzebub, 'this is fine. It's nice and hot in here. The Devil likes it here.'

35 Then they began the ridiculous old Christmas play that everybody knew so well. Beelzebub acted strongly, with lots of noise and humour. Fred played his part quite well, but at one

16

of the most important moments he forgot his lines. Arthur was nervous and awkward, so that Beelzebub had to help him with most of his part.

After lots of banging on pots which they carried, fighting with swords and falling on the floor, the play came to an end.   5
They waited in silence.

'Well, what next?' asked a voice from the shadows.

'It's your turn,' said Beelzebub.

'What do you want us to give you?'

'If your hearts are small, then give only a little,' laughed   10
Beelzebub.

'But,' said another voice, one they knew well. 'We have no heart to give at all.'

'You didn't know your lines very well,' said Blanche. 'The big fellow in the blanket deserves nothing.'   15

'What about me?' said Arthur.

'You,' answered the same voice. 'Oh, you are a nice boy, and a lady's thanks is enough reward for you.'

Arthur muttered something to himself and turned away.

'Well, you must pay the Devil,' said Beelzebub.   20

'Yes, give the Devil his reward,' laughed Blanche. Nellie threw a large silver coin on the floor, but she was nervous and it rolled away into the corner.

This was too much for Fred, dressed in his Arab's robes. He could bear no longer to stand looking ridiculous in front of the   25
lady he loved and her laughing friend.

He pulled off his robes, threw them over one arm, and with the other arm held back Beelzebub, who would have gone to pick up the money. There he stood, no longer an Arab, but a simple young farmer, with curly black hair, a stern look on his   30
face, and bare arms.

'Won't you let your brother have it?' asked Blanche. 'What do you want?' she asked.

'Nothing thanks. I'm sorry we troubled you.'

'Come on,' he said, pulling Beelzebub away, and the three of   35
them made their exit. Blanche laughed at them.

Nellie did not laugh. Seeing him turn, she saw him again as

17

a child, before her father had become rich, when she was a poor, simple little girl. After her father had made his money, selling cattle, their farm became one of the biggest in the area. He died, and she became the owner of the farm.

5 Nellie had seen little of her old friends since then. She had stayed a long time in town, and when she called on them after her return she found them cool and distant. So she had not visited them again, and now it was almost a year since she had spoken to Fred.

10 Just then Betty, the farm manager's wife, ran in excitedly.

'Look what I found. Look!' she exclaimed. It was a big bunch of shiny, green holly, thick with dark-red berries.

'Oh that is pretty,' said Blanche. 'Those boys must have brought it with them.'

15 Nellie looked a little uncomfortable. She rose and hurried down the passage to the sitting-room, followed by her friend. Then, to Blanche's surprise, she sat down and began to cry.

'Whatever is the matter?' asked Blanche.

It was some time before she had a reply. Then Nellie said,

20 'It's so miserable and lonely. I wish Willie and Harry and our other friends from town had come, then this wouldn't have happened. It was such a shame . . . such a shame.'

'A shame?' asked Blanche. 'What was?'

'Why, when he had gone to get the holly for me, and come

25 all this way to see me . . .' She ended, her cheeks turning pink.

'Whom do you mean. The Arab?'

'Now he will think I am just mean and proud.'

'What? Are you in love with him?'

Nellie began to cry again. 'I wish this farm and my money

30 had never come between us. He'll never come again, I know.'

'Then,' said Blanche, 'you must go to him.'

'Yes. And I will.'

Fred and Nellie

In the meantime the disappointed brothers had reached home. Fred had thrown his Arab robes down, and put on his coat, saying he was going to walk to the village. Then he had gone out. His mother's eyes watched him sadly, and his father looked at him without knowing what to say. However they heard him walk down the path and go into a barn where they kept tools and things, and they knew he would soon recover. 5 Arthur and Henry went to their room and soon nothing was heard in the house except for the tick of the clock.

In the barn it was black and cold. Fred sat on a bench staring out of the window. It was his own fault, he told himself and it was time to stop fooling himself about Nellie. She must 10 have thought he was foolish, and trying to chase after her because of her money. It was finished! What a fool he had been.

'But,' he argued. 'Let her think what she likes. I don't care. She probably doesn't even remember how I used to repair her 15 shoes with my father's leather, and how she had to borrow mine to go home.'

'But,' came the question, 'why doesn't she end it? I must be stupid to think she is even interested in me! She's more interested in those smart city boys. Well, what do I care!' 20

Suddenly he heard voices from the field behind the barn. Someone was behind the fence.

'Can we climb through here Blanche? There's a loose board here. Quietly now. We don't want anyone to see us!'

Nellie and Blanche crept past the barn towards the tiny 25 window, through which the kitchen light shone. They crouched down in front of a large bush near the window.

Fred made his way quietly out of the barn and hid behind the other side of the bush.

In the kitchen sat the father, smoking and appearing to 30 read, but really just staring into the fire. The mother was busy preparing some cakes.

'Oh Blanche,' whispered Nellie, 'he's gone out.'

'It looks like it,' she replied.

'Perhaps he's gone to his room.' 35

'Yes,' replied Blanche. 'He wouldn't want his mother to see him looking so miserable.'

21

'Certainly not,' said Nellie remembering how proud he was. Fred smiled to himself. Suddenly he felt very happy.

'But,' continued Nellie, 'if he has gone out, whatever shall we do? What can we tell his mother?'

5 'Let's just tell her we came here for fun.'

'But if he is out?'

'We can wait till he comes back,' Blanche replied firmly.

'But what if he comes back late? How long can we wait?'

'Well, it's Christmas Eve.'

10 'Perhaps he doesn't care after all.'

'You think he does, so do I; and you are quite sure you want him?'

'You know I do Blanche, and I always have.'

'Well, let's begin singing some Christmas carols* then.'

15 The girls began to sing a sweet Christmas carol. The mother and father looked up in surprise as the two voices suddenly began to sing outside. The mother wanted to run to the door, but her husband waved her back. 'Let them finish,' he said with his eyes shining. 'Let them finish.'

20 As Nellie sang she stood up and stepped so close to Fred that by leaning forward he could have touched her coat.

The girls finished. The door opened, showing a little woman holding out her hands.

Both girls made a move toward her, but . . .

25 'Nell, Nell,' Fred whispered, and caught her in his arms.

She gave a little cry of alarm and delight. Blanche stepped into the kitchen and shut the door, laughing.

Blanche sat down in a low chair, and chattered brightly about all sorts of things. And with a woman's eyes she noticed

30 the mother put her hands on her husband's as she sat on the sofa by his chair.

Soon the two came in, Nellie blushing. Without a word she ran and kissed the little mother and then turned to the quiet embrace of the father. Then she took off her hat and brushed

35 back the pretty curls from her face.

At last she was home.

*Christmas carol, a joyful song which is sung at Christmas.

3
A Shattered Dream

Muriel had sent me some flowers, some purple primroses, and some slightly faded, yellow honeysuckle*. They had arrived in a little cardboard box just as I was rushing off to school. 'Put them in water!' I said to Mrs Williams, my landlady, as I left the house. But those flowers had set my mood for the day. I   5
was dreamy and reluctant; school and the boys I had to teach were unreal, unsubstantial. What was real to me was those beautiful flowers that had arrived in the middle of a cold winter's day. The boys at school must have thought that I was an absent-minded fool. I regarded *them* as a punishment upon   10
me.

Memories of Muriel

I was glad when night came with the evening star, and the sky turned dark blue. I was as glad as if I were hurrying home to visit Muriel's house, as if she would open the door to me, and would invite me in to have tea. But when I got home, Eleanor,   15
the landlady's daughter, opened the door to me, and I poured my tea alone.

Mrs Williams had put my flowers in a vase on the table, and I thought of all the beautiful things we had done, Muriel and I, at home in the Midlands*. Of all the beautiful ways she had   20
looked at me, of all the beautiful things I had said to her . . . or had meant to say. I went on imagining beautiful things to say to her, while she looked at me with her wonderful eyes . . . Meanwhile I talked to my landlady about the neighbours.

Although I had a lot of work to do, I did not seem to be able   25
to do anything that night. Then I felt very miserable, and sat

---

honeysuckle, a climbing plant with sweet-smelling flowers. *the Midlands*, the middle part of England.

still and sulked*. At a quarter to eleven I said to myself, 'This will never do,' and I took my pen and wrote a letter to Muriel.

'It was not fair to send me those flowers. They have driven me crazy. Their little pinkish eyes follow me about, and I have
5 to think of you and home, instead of doing what I've got to do. All the time today while I was teaching at school my mind was elsewhere. The poor boys. I read their miserable pieces of composition over and over but I never really saw them. All I could think about was our last days together . . .'
10 I cannot remember at what time I finished my letter. I can recall a sensation of being dim, of having everything else out of my mind, smiling to myself as I sealed the envelope; of putting my books and papers in their places without the least knowledge of so doing. I cannot remember turning off the
15 electric light. The next thing I was conscious of was pushing at the kitchen door.

The youth

The kitchen is at the back of the house. Outside in the dark was a little yard and a tidy garden leading up to the railway tracks. I had come down the passage from my room in the
20 front of the house and stood pushing at the kitchen door to get a glass for some water. The kitchen was in darkness except for a few coals still burning red in the stove. Then I jumped. The shock was not quite enough to waken me fully. Pressing himself flat into the corner between the stove and the wall was a youth.
25 My mind was still far away, so I stood there looking and blinking my eyes.

'Why?' I said helplessly. I think my calmness must have terrified him. Immediately he began to edge out* and dodge* between the table and the stove, shouting viciously, snarling
30 like a dog.

'Don't touch me. Don't try to grab me. I'll hit you between

---

sulked, was silent and bad-tempered. **to edge out*, to move out slowly but not straight forward, rather at an angle and with caution. **dodge*, move about quickly keeping out of someone's way.

the eyes with this metal poker*. I haven't done anything to you. Don't touch me you coward!'

All the time he was writhing* about in the space where I had trapped him between the table and the stove. I was much too dazed to do anything but stare. Then my blood seemed to   5 change its quality. I became awake, sick and sharp with pain. I had seen boys behave like this in school and it disgusted me. I knew he did not dare strike.

'Stop your noise,' I said, standing still and stepping back a little. 'Do you want to wake the children?'   10

He had stopped writhing about and his voice sounded less violent.

'Put the poker down, you fool!' I pointed to the corner of the stove, where the poker used to stand. I supplied him with the definite idea of placing the poker in the corner, and in his   15 crazy state he could not reject it. He did as I told him, but as if he were not quite sure why he was doing it. The poker dropped to the ground with a clatter.

I looked at him, feeling him like a burden upon me, and in some way I was afraid of him for my heart began to beat   20 heavily. He crouched there like a cornered dog.

I took a box of matches and lit a gas light that hung in the middle of the bare little room. Then I saw that he was a youth of nineteen or so, with a thin face and narrow eyes. He was not ugly, nor did he look hungry. But he was clearly a labourer or a   25 worker of some sort. His hair had been cut close to his skull, making him look like a prisoner.

'I wasn't doing any harm,' he muttered, still trying to sound threatening. 'I haven't done anything to you. Leave me alone. What harm have I done?'   30

'Be quiet,' I said. 'You'll wake the children and the people in the house.'

I went to the door and listened. No one was disturbed. Then I closed the open window, which was letting in the cold, night air. I tried to think what to say to him.   35

*poker, a long, thin object used to push the wood or coal in a fire. *writhing, twisting or rolling oneself about; this can be caused by great physical or mental pain.

The boy was still standing in the same place. I sat down in a chair.

Two angry people

'What did you come in here for?' I asked almost pleadingly.
'Well,' he snapped back insolently. 'Wouldn't you if you had
5 nowhere to go on a cold night like this?'
'You came here to take something. What did you want from
here?' I looked around the kitchen unhappily. He looked back
at me uneasily, then at his dirty hands, then at me again. His
eyes looked miserable but cunning*.
10 'I might have taken some boots,' he said defiantly.
My heart sank. I hoped he would say, "food". Now I was
responsible for him. I hated him.
'You need a good thrashing*,' I said. 'We can hardly afford
to buy boots ourselves.'
15 'I've never done this before. This is the first time!'
'You miserable swine!' I said.
He looked at me with a flash of fury.
'Where do you live?' I asked.
'Exeter Road.'
20 'And you don't do any work?'
'I couldn't find a job, except . . . I used to deliver laundry.'
'And they threw you out for stealing?'
He moved a little uncomfortably. I did not press him.
'Who do you live with?'
25 'I live at home.'
'What does your father do?'
But he sat stubbornly and would not answer. I thought of
the gangs of youths who stood at the corner near the school.
They were always there, day after day, month after month,
30 insulting passers-by.
'But,' I said, 'what are you going to do with your life?'

---

cunning, clever at deceiving. *thrashing*, beating with a stick or whip.

He hung his head again and twitched uneasily. He could not answer.

'Are you going to marry a girl from the laundry, and live off her.' I asked sarcastically*.

He gave a sickly smile, evidently even a little bit flattered.   5 What was the use of talking to him?

'Or will you stand around the street corners until you go rotten?' I said.

He looked up at me sullenly*. 'Well, I can't get a job,' he snapped back. He was not hopeless, but like a man without   10 expectations, apathetic*, waiting to be provided for.

'Well, if you were a man, you would *find* a job,' I said. 'You'll *never* be a man!'

He grinned at me with sly insolence*, as if he knew something that I did not.   15

'And would any woman want to marry you?' I asked.

Then he grinned slyly to himself, ducking his head to hide the joke. And I thought of the coloured primroses and of Muriel's beautiful face. Then of him with his dirty clothes and his nasty skin! And that *he* would be a father one day!   20

'You don't know everything,' he sneered.

Despair

I sat and wondered. And I knew I could not understand him. I had no fellow feeling with him. He was something beyond me.

'Well,' I said helplessly, 'you'd better go.'   25

I rose, feeling he had beaten me. He could affect and alter me; I could not affect or alter him. He wandered off down the path. Then I shut the door.

In the silence of the sleeping house I stood quite still for some minutes, thinking about the fact of this man. I could not   30

---

sarcastically, saying something with the intention of hurting. *sullenly*, in a silently bad-tempered way. *apathetic*, without interest or feeling. *insolence*, a look which is insulting and shows no respect to another person.

accept him. I simply hated him. Then I climbed the stairs. It was like a nightmare. I could not get him out of my mind. As I hung up my coat, I felt Muriel's fat letter in my pocket. It made me feel a little sick. 'No!' I said, 'I don't want to think

5 of her.' And I wound up my watch sullenly, feeling alone and wretched.

28

4
Lessford's Rabbits

On Tuesday mornings I have to be at school early. It is my job to give out the free breakfasts to the children. Breakfast is at half past eight. The breakfasts are served in the woodwork room. I often arrive a few minutes late and have to hurry up the stairs. I generally find a little crowd of children waiting. I hurry through them to see if things are ready. There are two big girls putting out the bowls, and another one looking in a big pan to see if the milk is boiling. The room is warm, and seems more comfortable because the windows are high up near the roof and the walls are all varnished* and shining. Long tables are arranged in the shape of a U. The boys' bowls are placed around the outside, and the girls' on the inside. Then we are ready. Now I admit thirty children. They hurry to their places and stand in position, girls on the inside facing boys on the outside.

Free meals
  Last week the teacher who usually helps me did not come, so I was alone. She is an impressive-looking woman. I am always a little frightened of her. So I was quite relieved to find myself in charge without her. As I showed the children in, the caretaker, a fierce-eyed man with a large moustache, entered with the big basket full of bread. He looked around without saying good morning.
  'Miss Culloch not come?' he asked.
  'As you see,' I replied.
  He put down the basket, and left.
  I told one of the girls to give three pieces of bread to each child, and having taken a large insect out of the boiling milk, I

varnished, coated with a liquid which dries to a hard, shiny surface.

29

poured out each child's share of milk. Everything was ready. I
had to say a prayer. I could not think what to say. I did not
want to repeat what Miss Culloch used to say, thanking the
Lord for his goodness. I looked at the boys, dressed in other
5 children's old clothes, and the girls with their rat-tailed* hair.
We could thank the Lord for the good things in life, but who
were we supposed to thank for the bad things? I was becoming
desperate.

'Ready now, hands together, eyes closed. Let us eat, drink
10 and be merry, for tomorrow we die.' What did I mean?
Nobody seemed to care. There was the sound of thirty spoons
in the bowls, and a snuffling, slobbering sound of children
feeding. They were stretching wide their eyes and their mouths
at the same time, to get the spoon past their lips. They spilled
15 the milk on their clothes and wiped it off with their sleeves,
continuing to eat all the time.

'Don't spill your food children!' I said. They ate more
carefully, glancing up at me when the spoon was at their
mouths.

20 I began to count the children. There were only nine boys.
We could never get many boys to give their names for free
meals. I used to ask the Kellet children, who were thin and
hungry looking, 'Are you sure you don't want free breakfasts,
Kellets?'

25 The oldest boy would look at me curiously and say, with a
peculiar movement of his thin lips, 'No sir.'

'But do you have enough to eat?'

'Yes sir.' He was very quiet, embarrassed by my questions.

Very few of the boys wanted to accept the meals. Not many
30 parents wanted to have to be interviewed about their financial
situation, and about what they gave their children to eat. Most
boys would prefer to go hungry than to have to take free
breakfasts, which all their school friends would know about.

'Halket? Where is Halket?' I asked.

35 'Please sir, his mother has got a job and so he has

*rat-tailed, long and stringy like a rat's tail.

30

to stay at home to look after their baby,' replied Lessford.

Lessford

Lessford was one of the boys in my own class. He was a pink-faced, healthy little boy. Many of those at breakfast *did* look healthy. Lessford was brown-skinned and had fine dark eyes. He was a shy creature, who could neither spell, read nor draw, but who sometimes managed arithmetic. I think he came from a very poor family. He had an irritating habit of looking at me out of the corner of his eyes. He was a well-built boy and wore a blue jersey with big holes at the elbows. At breakfast he was a great eater. He would have five big pieces of bread, and then ask for more.

We gave them bread and milk one morning, cocoa and cake the next. I happened to take charge one cocoa morning. Lessford, I noticed, did not eat nearly as much as he did on bread mornings. I was surprised. I asked him if he did not like cake, but he said he did. Feeling curious, I asked the other teachers what they thought of him. Mr Hayward, who often was in charge of the cocoa and cake mornings, said he was sure the boy ate breakfast before he came to school. Mr Jephson, who took a bread and milk morning, said the boy had a huge appetite, and that it amused him to try to fill him up. I decided to watch him closely, turning suddenly to ask if anyone wanted a little more milk, and glancing over the top of the milk pan as I was emptying it.

I caught him! I saw him push a piece of bread under his jersey, looking carefully to see if anyone was watching him. I pretended not to have seen it, but when he was going downstairs I followed him and asked him to go into the classroom with me. He stood with his eyes to the floor, scratching the floor with his foot. He came to me, very slowly, when I asked him to step forward. I put my hand on his jersey and felt something underneath it. I pulled it out. It was his cap. He smiled and I felt foolish. I tried again, and this time I found three pieces of bread inside a rough pocket in the waist of his trousers. He looked at them sadly as I arranged them on the table in front of him.

'What does this mean?' I asked. He hung his head and would not answer. 'You may as well tell me. What do you want this
5   for?'

'Eat,' he muttered, keeping his face bent. I put my hand under his chin and lifted up his face. He shut his eyes, and tried to move his face aside, as if from a very strong light which hurt him.
10   'That is not true,' I said. 'I know perfectly well it is not true. You have breakfast before you come. You do not come to eat. You come to take food away!'

'I do not!' he exclaimed.

'No,' I said. 'You did not take any yesterday. But the day
15   before you did.'

'I did not. I did not.' He declared more firmly.

I thought again. 'Oh no. The day before was Sunday. Let me see. You took some on Thursday . . . yes, that was the last time. You took four or five pieces of bread.' I did not say
20   anymore. Nor did he. He scraped his toe along the ground. I had guessed right. He could not deny it, now that I seemed to know the exact amount he had taken.

But I could not get another word from him. He stood and heard all I had to say, but he would not look up, nor answer
25   anything. I felt angry.

'Well,' I said. 'If you come to any more breakfasts, you will be reported.'

He was a funny boy. He always came to school with dirty boots. It seemed that he was always wandering over the fields.
30   Halket was his great friend. But they never played together at school and they did not seem to have any common interest. Halket was a smart looking boy, and clever, but one of those you thought might well end up getting himself in trouble. He was quick to show his emotions, and would quickly go from
35   tears to laughter. Lessford was a quiet, sulking boy. Yet they always went around together.

The rabbits disappear

One day Lessford arrived at half past two. He was sweating and untidy and breathing heavily. He did not explain why he was late, but stood near the blackboard, his head dropped, legs loosely apart, breathing loudly.

'Well,' I exclaimed. 'What do you want to tell me?' I rose 5
from my chair.

It seemed that he had nothing to say.

'Come on!' I said. 'Don't fool with me. Let me hear it.'

He knew he would have to speak. He looked up at me, his dark eyes blazing. 10

'My rabbits have all gone!' he cried, just as a man would speak telling his wife that his children had been killed. I heard Halket give out a cry. I looked at him. He was standing half out of his desk, his face white with shock.

'Who took them?' asked Halket breathing the words almost 15
in a whisper.

'Did you leave the door open?' Lessford bent forward like a snake that was about to strike as he asked this. Halket shook his head.

'No! I haven't been near them today.' 20

There was a pause. It was time for me to do something. I told them both to sit down, and we continued the lesson. Halket crept near his friend and began to whisper to him, but he received no reply. Lessford sat sadly, not moving his head for more than an hour. 25

At playtime I began to question Halket.

'Sir we had some rabbits in a place near our house. A neighbour used to let us keep them in his toolshed you see . . .'

'How many did you have?'

'We had two brown females, : nd a black male. Sometimes 30
there were as many as sixteen young ones.'

I was somewhat surprised to hear this. 'How long have you had them?' I asked.

'A long time, sir. We have had six lots of young ones.'

'And what did you do with them?' 35

'Fatten them sir.' He sounded quite proud, but he did not

want to say too much. He waited for the next question.

'And what did you fatten them with?'

The boy looked quickly at me. His face reddened, and he became confused.

5 'Green stuff, that we took out of the gardens and the fields sir.'

'And bread?' I added quietly.

He looked at me. He saw I was not angry. For a few moments he hesitated, not sure whether to lie or not. Then he admitted
10 in a very quiet voice, 'Yes sir.'

'And what did you do with the rabbits?' He did not answer. 'Come, tell me.'

'We sold them sir.'

'Who sold them?'
15 'I did sir. To the grocer.'

'For how much?'

'Eighteen pence each.'

'And did your mothers know?'

'No sir.' He was very silent and guilty.
20 'And what did you do with the money?'

'We spent it. Going to the cinema.'

I asked him a day or two later if they had found the rabbits. They had not. I asked Halket what he thought had happened to them.
25 'I think someone must have stolen them sir. The door was not broken. You could open the lock easily with a knife. I suppose someone must have followed us that night when we fed them. I think I know who it is too, sir.'

Then he was silent again.

5
Rex

———

Every family has someone who does not belong, the black sheep
of the family as we say, and it seems that everyone too has at
least one *black* uncle. Sometimes even two! My mother's uncle
was our black uncle. My mother had loved him a lot when he
was a little boy, but when he grew older she said she would   5
never speak to him again. But actually when he did come
round to our house to visit us she always seemed quite pleased
to see him.

He arrived one day when I was a small boy. We viewed him
from a distance. He wanted us to look after a puppy for him.   10
Now my mother hated having animals around the house. She
could not bear the mix of human with animal life. Yet she
agreed to look after the pup.

My uncle had bought a large pub in a town not far away. It
was not a very fashionable place; quite the opposite.   15

I had to go and collect the pup. It was strange for me to
enter the big, noisy, smelly pub. It was called *The Good
Omen*. It was strange to see my uncle standing there in the
passage, shouting, 'Hello, Johnny, what do you want?' He did
not know me. Strange to think that he was my mother's   20
brother, and that at times he used to read literature!

The puppy
I had tea in a narrow, uncomfortable sort of living-room. I
was happy to leave a little later with the soft, fat pup. It was
winter time, and I wore a big black coat. I hid the puppy under
it. I was trembling. It was Saturday, and the train was   25
crowded, and the puppy whimpered under my coat. I was
frightened in case the train inspector found out about the
puppy and asked for my dog-ticket. However, we arrived, and
my fears were for nothing; no one challenged me.

35

The others were wildly excited over the puppy. He was small and fat and white with a brown and black head; a fox terrier. And he had a black spot just above the root of his tail.

It was Saturday night. We had just had our bath. He
5 crawled onto the rug like a fat white teacup and licked the bare toes that had just been bathed.

'He ought to be called Spot, because of the spot near his tail,' said one. But that was too ordinary. It was a great question, what to call him.

10 'Call him Rex, the King,' said my mother, looking down on the fat, wriggling little ball that was chewing my sister's toes and making her laugh. We all thought about the name seriously.

'Rex the King.' We thought it was just right. But it was not a
15 very successful name, really, because my father and all the people in the street failed completely to pronounce it correctly. They all said Rax. And it always annoyed me. Poor Rex!

We loved him dearly. The first night we woke to hear him weeping and crying in loneliness at the foot of the stairs. I
20 could not bear it, so I went downstairs for him, and he slept under the sheets.

'I won't have that little beast in the beds! Beds are not for dogs,' said my mother.

'He's as good as we are,' we replied, heart-broken.
25 'Whether he is or not, he's not going in the beds.'

The second night, however, Rex wept and in the same way he was comforted. The third night we heard our father walk heavily down the stairs. We heard several slaps and the yells of a sad puppy, and heard our father's heartless voice saying 'Stop
30 it then! Stop that noise. Get into your basket and stay there!'

'It's a shame,' we shouted from our bedroom.

'Be quiet and go to sleep,' called our mother from her room. We burst into tears and went to sleep.

'What fools you all are. It makes me hate him even more,
35 when you make such a fuss over him,' said mother.

But actually, she did not hate Rex at all. She only had to pretend to, to stop us loving him too much. In fact she did not like being too close to animals. My father, however, used to talk in a dog's voice, to the puppy. It was a funny, high, sing-song voice which he seemed to produce at the top of his head. 'Such a pretty little dog. Ah yes. Ah yes! Show me how you can wag your tail now, Rexie. There, that's right.' The puppy by now was wild with excitement and licked my father's nose, biting him with his sharp little teeth.

'That will teach you a lesson for being so silly with him,' said mother. It was strange to see her as she watched my father, crouching on the floor and talking to the little dog and laughing strangely when the little creature bit his nose. What does a woman think of her husband at such a moment!

My mother was always amused at the names we called him. 'He's an angel. He's a little butterfly. Rexie, my sweet!'

'Sweet! A dirty little object!' Mother exclaimed. She and Rex were at war from the very start. Of course he chewed boots and pulled at our socks and clothes. The moment we took our socks off he would run away with them, and we would run after him. Then as he pulled, growling loudly, at one end of the pair of socks and us at the other, we would cry:

'Look at him Mother. He'll make holes in them again.'

Then mother gave him a sharp slap.

'Let go, you naughty boy.'

But he did not let go. He began to growl in anger and hung on as tightly as he could. As small as he was, he was not going to give in to her. He did not hate her, nor she him. But they had one long battle with one another.

'I'll teach you, I will! Do you think I'm going to spend my life mending holes in socks?'

But Rexie only growled more viciously. They both became really angry, while we children pleaded with them both. He would not let her take the socks from him.

'You should tell him properly, Mother. You mustn't try to force him,' we said.

'I'll force him right out of this house. I *will*!' shouted Mother, truly angry. He would put her into a real temper, with his tiny, growling defiance. Every day there was trouble.

37

'He's sweet. Rexie. Little Rexie! Come here Rexie.'

'A dirty little nuisance. I won't put up with it.'

And to tell the truth, he was dirty at first. He could not help it. He was so young. But my mother hated him for it. And perhaps this was the real start of the problem. For he lived in the house with us. He would wrinkle his nose and show his tiny teeth when he was angry, and his battle-rage growls against my mother delighted us as much as they angered her.

Once she caught him making a mess on the floor. She picked him up, rubbed his nose in it, and threw him out into the yard. He yelped with shame and disgust and rage. I shall never forget the sight of him as he rolled over, then tried to turn his head away from the disgust of his own nose, shaking his little nose with a sort of horror and trying to sneeze it off. My sister gave a yell of pity and rushed out with a rag and a pan of water, weeping wildly. She sat in the middle of the yard with the puppy, and shedding bitter tears she wiped him and washed him clean. Loudly she called to my mother:

'Look how much bigger you are than he is. It's not fair. It's a shame.'

'You silly girl. You have undone all the good it would have done him, with your soft ways. Why is my life bothered with animals. Haven't I got enough to think about already?'

After that, everyone was quiet. Rex was a little barrier between us and our parents.

He became clean. But then another tragedy occurred. His tail had to be cut short! This time my father was the enemy. My mother agreed that it was an unnecessary cruelty. But my father was determined.

'The dog will look a fool all his life if his tail is not cut.' And to add to the horror, he said the best way to do it was to pay for a man to bite it off.

'Why?' we asked in horror.

It was the only way, we were told. A man would take the little tail and just bite it through gently with his teeth, at a certain joint. My father opened his mouth and pretended to do it. We shuddered. But there was nothing we could do.

38

Rex was carried away, and a man called Rowbotham, bit off his tail. We felt sorry for our poor little puppy, but we agreed that he looked better now. We would always have been ashamed of him if it had not been shortened. My father said it had made a man of him. 5

Good and bad

Perhaps it had. For now his true nature came out. And it seemed that there were two sides to him. First, he was a fierce, savage little beast. He loved to hunt, and he hunted cruelly. He loved to bite his teeth into somebody. He chased us when we annoyed him. He tried to attack anybody who came to the 10 house, especially the postman. He was almost a danger to the neighbourhood. But not quite. Because his second nature was the need to love. He had a terrible, terrible, necessity to love. So he was divided between two great desires; the desire to hunt and kill, and the strange, secondary desire to love and obey. If 15 he had been left to my mother and father, he would have run wild and got himself shot. But he loved us children with a fierce, joyous love. And we loved him.

When we came home from school, we would see him standing in front of the gate, with his little head twisted to one 20 side, looking out at the open spaces in front of him, and wondering whether to run off or stay. But as soon as one of us called his name from a far distance, like a bullet he threw himself down the road towards us. Seeing him coming, my sister always turned and ran, pretending that she was 25 frightened, shrieking with delighted terror. And he would jump straight up at her back, and bite her and tear her clothes. But it was only a game of love, and my sister knew it. She did not care if he tore her clothes but my mother did.

He made my mother furious. He was a little devil. And 30 whenever he could, he got into fights with her. If she wanted to sweep the floor, he jumped up and held onto the broom with his teeth. And he would not let go. With the hair around his neck standing up straight and the whites of his eyes staring at

39

my mother, she wrestled at the other end of the broom. 'Let go! Let go!' She pulled and twisted and stamped her foot, and he answered with a horrid growl. In the end it was she who had to let go. Then she flew at him and he flew at her. It seemed as if
5   he was almost going to bite her savagely. And she knew it. Yet he always kept sufficient self-control.

We children loved his temper. We would sometimes take away the bone he was eating, and put him into such a rage that he would turn his head right over and lie on the ground upside
10   down because he did not know what to do with himself. 'He'll go for your throat, one of these days,' said my father.

Neither he nor my mother would dare to try to touch one of Rex's bones. If they even came near him when he had a bone he would growl deeply and show the whites of his eyes. He must
15   have wanted to drive those teeth into us a hundred times. He was a horrid sight. But we only laughed and he would cry helplessly, unable to do anything.

He never did hurt us. He never hurt anybody, though everyone in the neighbourhood was terrified of him. But he
20   began to hunt. It disgusted my mother, because he would bring home large dead, bleeding rats and leave them on the rug. And mother had to pick them up with a shovel. For he would not remove them. Occasionally he brought home a rabbit that he had caught, and sometimes, a leg or a wing of a
25   chicken. We were frightened that the police would take him away. Once he came home bloody and feathery and looking very ashamed of himself. We cleaned him and questioned him and slapped him. Next day we heard of six dead ducks. Luckily no one had seen him.
30   But he was disobedient. If he saw a hen he would run off after it, and calling would not bring him back. He was worst of all with my father, who would take him for walks on Sunday morning. My mother never took him for walks. Once, walking with my father, he rushed off at some sheep in a field. My
35   father yelled at him, but he took no notice. The dog was in among the sheep and wanted to kill. My father finally caught him and began to beat him with a stick.

'That's very cruel,' said someone who was walking by.
'I mean it to be!' said my father.
The curious thing was that Rex did not respect my father at all, even after the beatings. But he always took notice of what we children said.   5

Rex disappears

But he let us down. One sad Saturday he disappeared. We hunted and called, but no Rex. We were bathed, and it was bedtime, but we would not go to bed. Instead we sat in our pyjamas on the sofa, and cried without stopping. This made our mother furious.   10

'I am not going to put up with it. I am not. And all this because of a horrible little dog. He *will* go.'

Our father came in late. He was a little drunk I think.

'Never mind,' he said. 'I'll look for him in the morning.'

Sunday came. Oh what a Sunday! We cried and we ate   15
nothing. We looked everywhere. My father walked for many miles. Nothing. When it was time for dinner, none of us could eat a thing.

'Never,' said my mother, 'never shall an animal set foot in this house again while I live. I knew it would be like this. I   20
knew!'

Night came and it was bedtime. Suddenly we heard a scratch and a little cry outside the door. In walked Rex, black with mud, and with a look that seemed to say, 'What's all the fuss about? Yes, I have come back. But I didn't have to. I can   25
look after myself remarkably well.'

Then he walked to his water, and drank noisily. He certainly knew how to deal with us!

He disappeared once or twice like this. We never knew where he went. And we began to feel that he was not the   30
perfect little creature we had imagined.

Then one awful day my uncle came back. He whistled to Rex and Rex trotted up to him. But when he wanted to have a closer look at the dog, Rex became suddenly still, then jumped free. He trotted round the room, but out of reach of my uncle. He leaped up, licking our faces and trying to make us play.

'Why, what have you done to this dog? You have made a fool of him. He is too soft. You have ruined him. You have made
5 him into a real fool!' shouted my uncle.

Rex goes home
Rex was captured and put into a box. He was desperate. He yelped and shrieked and struggled and was hit on the head with a stick by my uncle, which only made him more angry. So we saw him driven away, our beloved Rex, frantically trying to
10 escape, while we stood in the street not able to do a thing.

I saw Rex only once again, when I had to call at my uncle's pub, *The Good Omen*. He must have heard my voice, because he was there at the bottom of the stairs. And in an instant I knew how he loved us. He really loved us. And in the same
15 instant my uncle was there with a stick, beating him and kicking him back, and Rex was biting and snarling at him.

My uncle said many times that we had ruined the dog forever, spoiled him, and that he should never have left the dog with us. Poor Rex. We heard that his temper became
20 worse and worse and that he had to be shot!

And it was our fault. We had loved him too much, and he had loved us too much. We never had another pet.

It is a strange thing, love. Nothing but love has made the dog lose his wild freedom, to become the servant of man. And
25 yet while he serves man in total love, this very fact makes us see him as a disgrace. 'You dog,' we say.

We should not have loved Rex so much, and he should not have loved us.

We should have been crueller to him, and he should have
30 been crueller to us. Nothing is more fatal than the disaster of too much love. My uncle was right, we had ruined the dog.

My uncle was a fool, for all that.

6
The Princess

To her father, she was The Princess. To her aunts and uncles she was just Dollie Urquart. Her father, Colin Urquart, was just a bit mad. He was of an old Scottish family, and he claimed royal blood. His American relatives thought it was ridiculous. But he was a handsome man, with wide-open blue 5
eyes, soft black hair, good looks and a beautiful speaking voice that made people listen. He had sufficient money to be a man of class, to be well received and familiar in good society. He did not marry till he was nearly forty, a wealthy Miss Prescott, from New England. Hannah Prescott at twenty-two was 10
fascinated by the man with the soft black hair and the wide blue eyes. He was always charming, courteous, but he seemed oblivious* to things around him. Absent, almost.

The Princess is born

After a year Hannah gave birth to a little girl. But this did not change him. Perhaps it was that he was a little bit mad. 15
She thought it definitely the night her baby was born.

'Ah, so my little princess has come at last,' he said, in his deep singing voice.

It was a tiny little baby, with wise blue eyes. They called it Mary Henrietta. She called the little thing My Dollie. He called 20
it always My Princess.

Hannah Prescott had never been strong. She had no great desire to live. So when the baby was two years old she suddenly died.

Her parents felt a deep resentment against Colin Urquart. 25
They said he was selfish. They stopped sending any money, a month after Hannah's burial. The father refused to give them

*oblivious, unaware of.

43

his child. He simply treated them as if they were not there. He answered them. But of their actual existence he was never once aware.

5 They wanted to have him put in a hospital, to say that he was not mentally stable. But that would have created a scandal. So they ignored him. But they wrote regularly to the child, and sent her a little money at Christmas and on the anniversary of the death of her mother.

10 So the Princess lived with her father, and he travelled continually, though in a modest way, living on his moderate income. Italy. India. Germany. In each country the child changed nurses.

Father and child were inseparable. People called her Princess Urquart. She was a quick, dainty little thing with
15 dark-gold hair that went a soft brown, and wide blue eyes that looked at things deeply. She was always grown up. She never really grew up. Always strangely wise, and always childish.

A royal education
It was her father's fault.

'My little Princess must never take too much notice of people
20 and the things they say and do,' he repeated to her. 'People don't know what they are saying and doing. They talk, and they hurt one another, and they hurt themselves very often, till they cry. But don't take any notice, my little Princess. Because it is all nothing. They are not royal. Only you are royal, after
25 me. Always remember that. And always remember it is a great secret. If you tell people, they will try to kill you, because they envy you for being a princess. It is our great secret. And so darling, you must treat all people very politely. That is the way of royalty. But you must never forget that you alone are the last
30 of the princesses, and that all others are less than you are, less noble, more vulgar*. Never try to think of them as if they were like you. They are not. YOU are a princess.'

---

*vulgar, coarse and without good manners.

44

The Princess learned her lesson early. The first lesson was not to trust anybody but her family. The second was distant politeness towards everybody.

'She is so charming,' people would say. 'She is a real old-fashioned lady.' *5*

She stood very straight, but she was tiny beside her big, handsome, slightly mad father. She dressed very simply, usually in blue or grey. She had lovely little hands and a soft pink complexion. She looked as if she had stepped out of a picture; a picture that her father had painted. *10*

Her grandfather and grandmother and her Aunt Maud demanded to see her twice: once in Rome and once in Paris. Each time they were charmed, and also a little annoyed. She was so exquisite*, and at the same time so knowing and assured. But her grandfather was really fascinated. His wife *15* would catch him brooding over his grandchild, months after the meeting, and longing to see her again. He begged her to come and live with them.

'Thank you so much, grandfather. You are so very kind. But Papa and I are such an old couple, living in a world of our *20* own.'

Her father let her see the world from the outside. And he let her read. She read all the great writers, and seemed to under-stand them. Strange and uncanny, she seemed to understand things in a cold light, perfectly. This was her strength, and *25* sometimes it angered people. Taxi-drivers, workmen, who expected her to be soft, weak, and helpless if they spoke to her were at once put in their place by the cool and distant way she addressed them.

Encounters with such people made her tremble, and made *30* her know she must have support from the outside. The power of her spirit did not extend to these low people, and they had all the physical power. She knew they looked on her as a young and innocent woman, and when she rejected their aggressive masculinity, they hated her. She felt their hatred. *35*

exquisite, very beautiful and almost perfect.

45

When she was nineteen her grandfather died, leaving her a considerable fortune, on the condition that she would live for six months of each year in the United States.

'Why should they make me conditions?' she said to her
5   father. 'I refuse to be imprisoned six months in the year in the United States. We will tell them to keep their money.'

'Let us be wise, my little Princess, let us be wise. Let us take their money, then they will not dare to be rude to us.'

There began a new phase, when the father and daughter
10 spent their summers in California, or in the South-west. The father was something of a poet, the daughter, something of a painter. He wrote poems about the lakes or the redwood trees, and she made dainty drawings. He was physically a strong man, and he loved the out-of-doors. He would go off with her
15 for days, paddling in a canoe and sleeping by a camp-fire. She would ride with him on horseback over the mountain trails till she was so tired she was nothing but a body sitting on her pony. But she never gave in.

People said to her as the years passed, and she was a woman
20 of twenty-five, then a woman of thirty, and always the same dainty Princess, 'Don't you ever think what you will do when your father is no longer with you?'

'No I never think of it,' she said, looking coldly at the questioner.

25 She had a tiny, but beautiful little house in London, and another in Connecticut, with a housekeeper in each. And she knew many literary and artistic people. What more?

So the years passed. She never seemed to change. At thirty-three she looked twenty-three. Her father, however, was aging,
30 and becoming stranger. He spent the last three years of his life in the house in Connecticut. He became violent as his condition worsened, and he sometimes threatened the Princess with violence. Physical violence was horrible to her. It seemed to shatter her heart. But she found a kind woman to be a sort
35 of nurse-companion to the mad old man. So the fact of madness was never openly admitted.

Alone in the world

The Princess was thirty-eight years old and quite unchanged when her father died. She was still tiny, and like a dignified, scentless flower. Her fluffy hair bobbed around her apple-blossom* face. From her blue eyes she looked out with her eternal challenge. She was the Princess, and sardonically* she looked out on a Princess world.   5

She was relieved when her father died, and at the same time, it was as if everything had evaporated around her. What was she to do? She seemed faced with absolute nothingness. She had only her father's companion, Miss Cummins, who shared   10 with her the secret, and almost the passion of her father. And now Miss Cummins was the vessel that held the passion for the dead man. She herself, the Princess, was an empty vessel. An empty vessel in the enormous warehouse of the world.

She felt that she must *do* something. Never, never before   15 had she felt like that, that she must *do* something. That was left to the vulgar.

But now that her father was dead, she found herself on the fringe of the vulgar crowd, sharing their necessity to *do* something. It was a little humiliating. She found herself   20 looking at men more closely and thinking about marriage. Not that she felt any sudden interest in men, or attraction towards them. No. But *marriage*, that peculiar abstraction, had imposed a sort of spell on her. That was the thing she ought to do.   25

Her father had died in the summer, the month after her thirty-eighth birthday. When all was over, the obvious thing to do, of course, was to travel with Miss Cummins. The two women knew each other intimately, but at a distance. Miss Cummins had a sort of passionate respect for the Prinesss, who   30 seemed to her, ageless, timeless. Miss Cummins too had never married, had never known a man. Her skin was pale and clear, but there was a certain blankness in her expression.

---

apple-blossom, pinkish-white, like the flower of the apple tree. *sardonically*, with scornful laughter.

The Princess did not want to go to Europe. Her face turned West. She wanted to go to New Mexico. So she and Miss Cummins arrived at the Rancho del Cerro Gordo towards the end of August, when the crowd was beginning to drift back East. The ranch lay by a stream on the desert some four miles from the foot of the mountains. It was a ranch for the rich. She and Miss Cummins had a little cottage each but took dinner together in the evenings in the large guest-house. For the Princess still entertained the idea of marriage.

Looking for a husband

The guests at the Rancho del Cerro Gordo were of all sorts, except the poor sort. They were practically all rich, and many were romantic. Some were charming, others were vulgar. So the Princess talked a great deal with those who seemed interesting. She painted with the artists, and rode with the young men from college, and had altogether quite a good time. However marriage still remained completely in the abstract. Not connecting it with any of these young men, even the nice ones.

The Princess looked just twenty-five. When she was *forced* to write her age, she wrote twenty-eight, making the figure *two* rather badly, so that it just avoided being a three. Men hinted marriage at her. Especially boys from college suggested it from a distance. But the only man who intrigued her at all was one of the guides, a man called Domingo Romero. It was he who had sold the ranch itself to the Wilkiesons, ten years before, for two thousand dollars. He had gone away, then reappeared at the old place. For he was the son of the old Romero, the last of an old and famous Spanish family that had owned miles of land around San Cristobal. Today their descendants were just Mexican peasants.

Domingo, the heir, had spent his two thousand dollars, and was working for white people. He was now about thirty years old. He was a tall, silent fellow, with a heavy, closed mouth and black eyes that looked across at one almost sullenly. From

48

behind he was handsome, with a strong, natural body. But his dark face was long and heavy, almost sinister* but with a look like that of many Mexicans of his own locality, waiting either to die or to be aroused into passion and hope.

Domingo Romero was almost a typical Mexican to look at, with the typical heavy, dark, long face, clean-shaven, with an almost brutally heavy mouth. His eyes were black and Indian-looking. Only at the centre of their hopelessness was a spark of pride, or self confidence.

But this spark was the difference between him and the mass of men. It gave him a certain beauty. Silent, aloof, he was an admirable guide, with a startling quick intelligence that anticipated difficulties before they arose. He could cook too, crouching over the camp-fire and moving his slim brown hands. He was never chatty* or friendly however. Some of the tourists did not like him as a guide. 'One can't get any response from him,' they said. They never saw the spark in the middle of Romero's eye. They were not alive enough to see it.

The Princess caught it one day, when she had him for a guide. And instantly she knew that he was a gentleman. And instantly her manner towards him changed.

They were fishing, and he had perched her on a rock over a quiet pool. It was early September. The canyon was already cool, but the leaves of the trees were still green. The Princess stood on a rock, wearing a soft grey sweater and neatly cut trousers, with high black boots; her fluffy brown hair worn under a little grey hat. She knew perfectly well how to handle a fishing line.

Romero, in a black shirt and with loose black trousers, was fishing a little further down the river. He had caught three trout. From time to time he glanced up-stream at the Princess. He saw that she had caught nothing.

Soon he quietly drew in his line and came up to her. He watched her closely, quietly suggesting certain changes to her, putting his sensitive brown hand before her. And he withdrew

*sinister, evil looking. *chatty, fond of talking.

49

a little, and stood in silence, leaning against a tree, watching her. She knew it, and was thrilled. And in a moment, she had a bite*. In two minutes she had landed a good trout. She looked round at him quickly, her eyes sparkling. And as she met his 5 eyes a smile of greeting went over his dark face. Her cheeks flushed, and her blue eyes darkened.

After this, she always looked for him. A vague, unspoken intimacy grew up between them. She liked his voice, his appearance, his presence. There was a certain correctness in 10 his appearance. He was always perfectly shaved, his hair was always in place. He seemed elegant, slender, yet he was very strong. And at the same time, he gave her the feeling, curiously, that death was not far from him. Perhaps he too was half in love with death.

15 Small as she was, she was quite a good horsewoman and every day the Princess set off with Miss Cummins and Romero, on horseback, riding into the mountains. She had never felt as comfortable in Romero's presence as she had with any white man. He had a strange power to help her in silence across a 20 distance, if she were fishing without success, or if her horse became scared. She had never known this before, and it was thrilling.

And yet she never thought about *marriage* when she was with him. For some reason, in her strange little brain, the idea 25 of marrying him was unthinkable. Not for any definite reason. It was as if their souls were already married, but their outer selves, Miss Urquart and Señor Domingo Romero, could never marry.

The time passed, and she let it pass. The end of September 30 came, and the trees began to change colour.

'When will you go away?' Romero asked her, looking at her fixedly with a blank black eye.

'By the end of October,' she said, 'I have promised to be in Santa Barbara at the beginning of November.' She saw a 35 thickening of his heavy mouth and turned away from him.

---

*had a bite, had a fish on the end of a fishing line.

50

She had complained to him many times that one never saw any wild animals. A few squirrels, perhaps, but never a deer or a bear.

'Yes,' he said. 'There are deer, and bear. But it's hard for you to see them. You have to keep still, in a place where they come. Do you want to go up into the mountains or some place, to wait till they come?'

As he spoke a smile came suddenly to his face.

'Yes,' she said.

'Well,' he said, 'you will have to find a house. It's very cold at night now. You would have to stay up all night in a house.'

'Are there no houses up there?' she said.

'Yes,' he replied. 'There is a little shack* that belongs to me. A miner built it a long time ago. You can go there and stay one night. Maybe you'll see something.'

'Is there water there?' she asked.

'Yes, there is a pond, you know, below the spruce trees.'

'Is it far away?' she asked.

'Yes, pretty far. You see that ridge there,' and turning to the mountains he lifted his arm in gesture to the distance.

'I should like to go,' she said.

'I know Mrs Wilkieson will be mad with me if I take you up in the mountains to that place. I'll have to go there first, to take lots of blankets and some food. Maybe Miss Cummins won't be able to stand it. It's a hard trip.'

He was speaking and thinking in the heavy, disconnected, Mexican fashion.

'Never mind,' said the Princess decisively. 'I will arrange with Mrs Wilkieson and we'll go on Saturday.'

But he explained that they could not leave before Monday, so they agreed to start on Monday morning at seven. The obedient Miss Cummins was told to prepare for the trip. The Princess was in high spirits when Monday arrived. As she was dressing, she saw him bringing in three horses.

The night had been cold and there was ice on the ground.

*shack, a hut which is roughly built.

51

'We may be away two or three days,' she explained to Mrs Wilkieson.

'Very well,' said Mrs Wilkieson. 'Romero will look after you. You can trust him.'

The journey

5   The sun was already on the desert as they set off towards the mountains. The cottonwood trees behind the ranch were yellowing under the perfect blue sky. The three trotted gently along the trail, towards the sun that sparkled yellow just above the mountains. The canyon was full of a deep blueness. They
10   rode single file; Romero first, on a black horse. The Princess came next and Miss Cummins, who was not very comfortable on horseback, came last, in a pale dust that the others kicked up. Sometimes her horse sneezed, and she jumped.

Romero never looked round. He could hear the sound of the
15   hoofs following, and that was all he wanted. They neared the foot-hills and rode up a steep, stony slope. Then they dropped into the shadow of the San Cristobal canyon where a stream was running full and swift.

It was dark and cool as the horses climbed upwards. They
20   were quite high now. The Princess rode on after Romero. Then came a great crashing behind. The Princess was aware of Romero's dark face looking round, before she herself looked round, to see Miss Cummins' horse scrambling up from the rocks with one of its knees already red with blood.

25   'He almost went down,' called Miss Cummins.

But Romero was already out of the saddle and running down the path. He began examining the cut knee.

'Is he hurt?' cried Miss Cummins anxiously, and she climbed hastily down.

30   'Not very badly,' said Romero. 'Nothing broken.'

Again he bent down and worked at the knees. Then he looked up at the Princess.

'He can go on,' he said. 'It's not bad.'

'How many hours more?' asked Miss Cummins.

52

'About five,' said Romero, simply.

'Five hours,' cried Miss Cummins. 'And a horse with a wounded leg. I would not think of it. I wouldn't ride him up there. Not for all the money in the world.'

Romero bent down to the horse's knee again.   *5*

'Maybe it hurts him a little,' he said. 'But he can make it.'

'I know it hurts him. Oh, I just couldn't bear it.'

'But Miss Cummins, dear, if Romero says he'll be all right,' said the Princess.

They were unable to change Miss Cummins' mind.   *10*

'Well,' said Romero. 'I guess we go back then.'

'No,' cried the Princess. Her voice rang with disappointment and anger.

Miss Cummins rose with energy.

'Let me lead the horse home,' she said with cold dignity,   *15* 'and you two go on.'

This was received in silence. The Princess was looking down at her with a cold almost cruel gaze.

'We've only come about two hours,' said Miss Cummins. 'I don't mind walking him home. But I couldn't ride him. I   *20* couldn't.'

'Very well then,' said the Princess. 'You lead him home. You'll be quite all right. And say to them that we have gone on and will be home tomorrow, or the day after.'

She spoke coldly and distinctly.   *25*

Then Romero spoke. 'If you want,' he said, 'I'll go on with you. But first Miss Cummins can ride my horse to the end of the canyon, and I'll walk beside her with her horse. Then I'll come back to you.'

It was arranged so. Miss Cummins had her saddle put on   *30* Romero's black horse, and they started back. The Princess rode on very slowly, alone. She was so angry with Miss Cummins that she forgot everything else. She just let her horse follow the track. Her horse walked steadily all the time. They emerged after a while on a bare slope, and the trail wound   *35* through thin aspen trees. She paused and looked back. The near great slopes sparkled with gold, and away through the gap

in the canyon she could see the pale blue of the desert.

On the trail

She was going on alone with Romero, but she was very sure of herself. Romero was a man to be trusted. She wanted to go on with him; there was some peculiar link between the two of
5   them. She rode on and came to a flat little valley of quiet-standing yellow aspen trees from which the stream poured into the lower rocks of the canyon. Here she was to wait for Romero, and they were to have lunch.

She unfastened her saddle and pulled it to the ground with a
10   crash, letting her horse wander with a long rope. She took out the packages of lunch, spread a little cloth, and sat to wait for Romero. She made a little fire and ate an egg. Then she sat in the sun, in the stillness near the trees, and waited. The sky was blue. Beyond and up jutted the great slopes of the mountains.
15   Then she saw her horse jump and begin to run. Two ghost-like figures on horseback appeared from the trees across the stream. It was two Indians, wrapped in grey blankets. Their guns jutted beyond the saddles. They rode straight towards her, to her thread of smoke. As they came near they greeted
20   her, looking at her curiously with their dark eyes. Their long black hair was somewhat untidy. They looked tired. They got down from their horses near her little fire and walked towards her. One was a young Indian she had met before, the other was an older man.
25   'You all alone?' said the younger man.

'Romero will be here in a minute,' she said, glancing back along the trail.

'Ah, Romero. You with him? Where are you going?'

'Round the ridge*,' she said. 'Where are you going?'
30   'We're going down to Pueblo.'

'Been out hunting? How long have you been out?'

'Yes. Been out five days.' The young Indian gave a

*ridge, long narrow hill-top.

56

DH LAWRENCE

meaningless laugh. The Princess was not afraid.

'Got anything?'

'No. We saw two tracks of deer — but got nothing.'

'You must have been cold,' she said.

'Yes, very cold in the night. And hungry. Had nothing to eat   5
since yesterday.' And again he laughed his meaningless laugh.

Under their dark skins, the two men looked hungry. The
Princess opened her saddle-bag and took out some bacon and
bread. She gave them this, and they began toasting slices of it
on long sticks at the fire.   10

Just then Romero rode up, his face expressionless. The
Indians greeted him in Spanish. He unsaddled his horse, took
food from the bags, and sat down at the camp to eat. The
Princess went to the stream for water, and to wash her hands.
They lingered a while, then Romero saddled the horses. The   15
Indians still squatted* by the fire. Romero and the Princess
rode away, calling, 'Goodbye,' in Spanish to the Indians.

When they were alone, Romero turned and looked at her
curiously, in a way she could not understand. And for the first
time she wondered if she was wise to travel alone.   20

'I hope you don't mind going on alone with me,' she said.

'If you want to,' he replied.

The trail was almost invisible. Slowly they climbed the slope,
the wind rushing against their faces. For an hour their horses
rushed up the slope of the mountain, halting to breathe from   25
time to time, scrambling again, then forcing up, length by
length. All was grey and dead around them. Nothing grew
here. But they were near the top now, near the ridge. Even the
horses made a rush for the last bit. Then they were over the
crest at last. In front now was nothing but massive mountains.   30
Here and there were patches of white snow. It frightened the
Princess. It was so inhuman. She had not thought it could be so
inhuman. And yet now one of her desires was fulfilled. She had
seen it; the massive core of the Rockies*. The gigantic

---

*squatted, crouched down near the ground with knees bent. *the Rockies, a range of
mountains in the west of North America.

mountains frightened her and she wanted to go back. At this moment she wanted to turn back but Romero was riding on. He turned round to her and pointed at the slope with a dark hand.

5   'Look. Here a miner has been digging for gold,' he said. It was a grey scratched-out heap near a hole, as if an animal had been digging there.

'Quite recently?' said the Princess.

'Not long ago—twenty, thirty years.'

Afraid!

10   They worked along the ridge, up and down. It was cold. The Princess was afraid. For one moment she looked out, and saw the desert, shining pale and vast, far below. It was terrifying. To the left was the mass of mountains all kneeling heavily.

She closed her eyes and let her consciousness leave her. The

15 horse followed the trail. So on and on, in the wind again, they began to descend. The horses slithered* on the loose stones, picking their way downwards. It was afternoon and the air was getting colder. She was barely conscious at all of Romero until she felt him close to her side, lifting her off her horse.

20   'We must slide down here,' he said. 'I can lead the horses.'

'No,' she said. 'I will take my horse.'

'Then be careful he doesn't slip down on top of you,' said Romero. He led the way, going from rock to rock, down the pale, steep incline. His horse hopped and slithered after him,

25 and sometimes stopped dead, with forefeet pressed back, refusing to go farther. Romero, below his horse, looked up and pulled the reins gently, and encouraged the creature. Then the horse once more dropped his forefeet with a jerk, and the descent continued.

30   The Princess followed as best she could, with Romero constantly looking back to see how she was doing. She looked as frail and delicate as a bird's egg but she managed alone.

slithered, slid awkwardly.

58

At last they were down. Romero sat in the sun, out of the wind, beside some bushes. The Princess came near, the colour flaming in her cheeks, her eyes dark blue and glowing unnaturally.

'We made it,' said Romero.   5

'Yes,' said the Princess, dropping onto the grass, unable to speak, unable to think. In a few minutes her consciousness and her control began to come back. She drank a little water. Romero was attending to the saddles, then they were off again. And after they had ridden for an hour, through crowded trees,   10 they emerged. And there under the sun was a little cabin, and the bottom of a small naked valley with a grey rock and heaps of stones, and a round pool of intense green water. The sun was just about to leave it. Indeed, as she stood, the shadow came over the cabin and over herself: they were in the gloom of   15 twilight. Above, the heights still blazed.

At the cabin

It was a little wooden cabin, near the spruce trees, with an earthen floor, and an unhinged door. There was a wooden bed-bunk, three wooden stools, and a sort of fireplace. No room for anything else.   20

Romero set a little fire going and went out to attend to the ' horses. The Princess sat there on one of the wooden stools in front of the fire, warming her tiny hands at the blaze. She was in a sort of daze.

'You will have some tea now? Or wait for some soup?'   25 Romero asked.

'Some tea,' she said. She followed him into the open. Their horses were cropping the grass among the stones. Romero carried the cooking things and blankets into the cabin. The Princess went down the stones to the water. It was very still and   30 mysterious, and of a deep green colour, yet pure, transparent as glass. How cold the place was. How mysterious. Suddenly she saw eyes like sparks, gazing at her across the water. It was a wild-cat, crouching by the water's edge and it was watching her with cold, electric eyes shining in the darkness.

She made a swift movement, spilling her water. And in a flash, the creature was gone, leaping like a cat that is escaping; but strange and soft in its motion, with its little tail behind it.

5 She went back into the cabin. Romero came in with an armful of twigs for the fire. 'We burn these,' he said. 'They hardly make any smoke.'

Curious and remote he was, saying nothing except what had to be said. And she, for her part, was as remote from him.

10 They seemed far, far apart, worlds apart, now they were so near.

'You lie down and rest,' he said. 'I'll make supper.'

Soon she could smell the soup he was heating. He handed her the first cupful. She sat among the blankets, drinking it

15 slowly. Then he gave her a plate with pieces of fried chicken. It was very good. She did not say a word. She felt he had a power over her. A certain resentment filled her. After she had eaten she went out into the night. What she was frightened of, she did not know. Romero approached her.

20 'You don't want to go away from here,' he said. 'This is a nice place.'

She shrank back from him.

'Come,' he said, taking her gently by the arm in a powerful grasp. Quietly he led her back and seated himself by the

25 doorway, still holding her by the arm.

A test of wills

'Look, this is a nice place. You are such a pretty white woman. I want you to like me. I'm not going to let you go. I reckon you called me here. If you say you want to be with me, we'll go down to the ranch tomorrow and get married or

30 whatever else you want. But you've got to say you want to be with me or I shall stay right here, till something happens.'

She waited a while before she answered.

'I don't want to be with anybody against my will. I don't dislike you; at least I didn't until you tried to put your will over

mine. I won't have anyone's will put over me. You can't
succeed. Nobody could. You can never marry me against my
will.'

He thought about what she said, and she regretted having
said it. Then, sombre*, he went back to the cooking again. He   5
could not conquer her, because her spirit was as hard and
flawless as a diamond. But he could shatter her. This she knew
and what was more, she *would* be shattered.

'Where are you going to sleep?' she asked.

'I make my bed here,' he pointed to the floor along the wall.   10
'Too cold outside.'

'Yes,' she said. 'I suppose it is.'

She sat immobile, her cheeks hot, her head full of conflicting
thoughts. And she watched him while he folded the blankets
on the floor, a sheepskin underneath.   15

'What about the horses?' she said.

'My black won't go away. And your mare will stay with him.'

He blew out the lantern, and sat down on his bedding. She
lay with her back turned. What did she want? She thought to
herself. Did she really want to marry this man? She could hear 20
the steady breathing of the sleeping man. She wanted to be
taken away from herself. And at the same time, perhaps more
deeply than anything, she did not want anyone to have power
over her. It was a wild necessity in her that no one, particularly
no man, should have any rights or power over her, that no one   25
and nothing should possess her.

She fell asleep, dreading the next day.

When dawn came, he was fast asleep. She sat up suddenly.
'I want a fire,' she said.

He opened his brown eyes wide. 'All right,' he said. 'I'll make 30
it.'

She could not bear to look at him.

'I suppose we will start back as soon as we've had breakfast?
Mrs Wilkieson will be expecting us.'

He was crouching at his camp-stove, making scrambled   35

sombre, looking or feeling miserable.

eggs. He looked up suddenly, a strange look on his face.

'You want to go?' he said.

'We'd better get back as soon as possible,' she said, turning aside from his eyes.

5 'You want to get away from me?' he asked.

'I want to get away from here,' she said decisively. And it was true. She wanted to get back to the world of people.

A prisoner

He rose and reached for her clothes that hung on a peg; her woollen jumper, her scarf and her riding boots. Sitting up she

10 saw him walk down to the dark-green pool in the frozen shadow of the deep cup of a valley. He threw the clothing and the boots into the pool. She sat in despair among the blankets, hugging them tightly around her.

'Now you'll stay with me,' he said.

15 She was furious. Her blue eyes met his. They were like two demons watching each other.

Then he pulled out her saddle, carried it to the pool and threw it in. He fetched his own saddle, and did the same.

'Now will you go away?' he said, looking at her with a smile.

20 She pulled the clothes over her head and broke into tears. She had never really cried in her life. He dragged the blankets away and looked to see what was shaking her. She sobbed in helpless hysterics. He covered her over again and went outside, looking at the mountains, where clouds were dragging and

25 leaving a little snow. It was a violent, windy, horrible day.

She cried for hours. After this a great silence came between them. He went about in silence. In the afternoon as she sat huddled in the doorway in the sun, wrapped in a blanket, she saw two horsemen come over the crest of the grassy slope. She

30 gave a cry. Romero looked up quickly and saw the figures. The men had climbed down off their horses and were looking for the trail down to the cabin.

He went and fetched his gun, and sat with it across his knees.

'Oh,' she said. 'Don't shoot. Please don't shoot.'

He looked across at her. 'Why?' he said. 'Do you like staying with me?'

'No,' she said. 'But don't shoot.'

'I'm not going to prison,' he said.

'You won't have to go to prison,' she said. 'Don't shoot.'   *5*

'I'm going to shoot,' he muttered.

And immediately he knelt and took very careful aim. The Princess sat on in an agony of helplessness and hopelessness.

The shot rang out. In an instant she saw one of the horses on the grassy slopes rear up and go rolling down. The man had   *10* dropped in the grass, and was invisible. The second man clambered on his horse and galloped towards the nearest trees for cover. Bang! Bang! went Romero's gun. But each time he missed, and the running horse leaped like a kangaroo towards cover*.   *15*

Romero now got behind a rock, tense and silent in the brilliant sunshine. The Princess sat on the bunk inside the cabin, crouching. For hours, it seemed, Romero knelt behind this rock, in his black shirt, bare-headed, watching. He had a beautiful alert figure. The Princess wondered why she did not   *20* feel sorry for him. But her spirit was hard and cold and her heart could not melt. Though now she would have called him to her, with love.

But no, she did not love him. She would never love any man. Never! It was fixed and sealed in her.   *25*

Rescued

Suddenly she was so startled she almost fell from the bunk. A shot rang out quite close from behind the cabin. Romero leapt straight into the air and even while he was in the air, a second shot rang out, and he fell with a crash, squirming, his hands clutching the earth towards the cabin door.   *30*

The Princess sat absolutely motionless, transfixed, staring at the outstretched figure. In a few moments the figure of a man

*cover, a place which gives shelter or protection from danger.

in the Forest Service appeared close to the house; a young man in a large hat, dark shirt, and riding boots, carrying a gun. He strode over towards the figure on the ground.

'Got you, Romero,' he said aloud. And he turned the dead
5 man over. There was already a little pool of blood on the ground. And he squatted, staring at the dead man. The distant calling of his comrade aroused him. He stood up.

'Hullo, Bill,' he shouted. 'Yeah. Got him.'

The second man rode out of the forest on a grey horse. He
10 had a kind face, and round brown eyes, but he looked saddened.

'You are sure he hasn't passed out,' he asked anxiously.

'No. He's dead all right,' replied the other.

Then he turned and looked into the cabin where the
15 Princess squatted, staring with big red eyes from under her blanket.

'What did he start firing for?' he asked.

She fumbled for words, with numb lips.

'He had gone out of his mind,' she said.

20 'Good lord. You mean to say he had gone mad? That explains it then.'

He seemed to accept her explanation and asked nothing more.

With some difficulty, they succeeded in getting the Princess
25 down to the ranch. But she too, was now a little mad.

'I'm not quite sure where I am,' she said to Mrs Wilkieson, as she lay on her bed. 'Do you mind explaining?'

Mrs Wilkieson explained tactfully.

'Oh yes,' said the Princess. 'I remember. And I had an
30 accident in the mountains, didn't I. Didn't we meet a man who had gone mad, and who shot my horse from under me?'

'Yes, you met a man who had gone out of his mind.'

After a fortnight, the Princess left the ranch and went East in Miss Cummins' care. Apparently she had recovered herself
35 entirely. She was the Princess again.

But her hair was now a little grey at the sides and her eyes were somewhat mad. She was slightly crazy.

'Since my accident in the mountains, when a man went mad
and shot my horse from under me, and my guide had to shoot
him dead, I have never felt quite well.'
So she put it.
Later she married an elderly man, and seemed pleased.   *5*

7
Adolf

Father

When we were children our father often worked at night. In spring he used to arrive home, black and tired, just as we came downstairs in our pyjamas. Poor Father, having to see us happily entering a new day as he was returning, dirty and
5 exhausted. He did not like going to bed in the spring morning sunshine.

But sometimes he was happy because of his long walk through the fields as the sun was coming up. He loved the early morning, after he had spent a night down the coal-mine. He
10 watched every bird, every movement of the grass, and if he could, he would have called and whistled to the birds in a secret language. He liked non-human things best.

One sunny morning we were all sitting at the table when we heard his heavy footsteps coming up the path. It made us feel
15 nervous. He passed the window and we heard him go into the back of the house. Then he came into the kitchen. We felt at once that he had something to communicate. No one spoke. We watched his black face for a second.

'Give me a drink,' he said.
20 My mother hastily poured out his tea. But instead of drinking it he suddenly put something down on the table among the teacups. A tiny brown rabbit! A small rabbit sitting against the bread as if it were made of china.

'A rabbit! A young one! Who gave it to you, Father?'
25 But he laughed and went to take off his coat. We picked it up excitedly.

'Is it alive? Can we feel its heart beat?'

My father came back and sat down. He took a slow sip from his tea.
30 'Where did you find it?'

'Is it a wild one?' asked my mother.

'Yes it is,' he replied without looking at her.
'Then why did you bring it?' cried my mother.
'Oh we wanted it,' came our cry.
'Yes, I've no doubt you did,' Mother replied. We fired our
questions at Father.   5
On the path through the fields my father had found a dead
mother rabbit and three dead little ones and this one alive, but
not moving.
'What had killed them, Daddy?'
'I don't know. I think the Mother had eaten something.'   10
'Why did you bring it!' Mother shouted angrily. 'You know
what a nuisance it will be.'
My father made no answer, but we were quick to disagree.
'He had to bring it. It's not big enough to live by itself. It
would die,' we shouted.   15
'Yes, and it will die now.'
We looked at Father sadly.
'It won't die, Father, will it? Why will it? It won't.'
'I don't think so,' said my father.
'You know it will. We've been through all this before,' said   20
my mother.
She reminded him of other little wild animals he had
brought home, which had refused to live and brought tears to
us all.

The rabbit is saved
The little rabbit sat sadly on our laps, still, its eyes wide and 25
dark. We brought it milk, warm milk, and held it to its nose. It
sat as still as if it were far away, hidden under the ground
perhaps. We wet its mouth with drops of milk. It gave no sign.
It did not even shake off the wet white drops. Somebody began
to cry.   30
'I told you,' cried my mother. 'Take it and put it back in the
field!'
But nobody wanted to do that. We hurried to get dressed for
school. There sat the rabbit. It was like a tiny cloud. It was

better not to try to love it. If it died we would be sad. So I passed the order to my sister and my mother. The rabbit was not to be spoken to, nor even looked at. Wrapping it in a piece of cloth, I put it out in the room at the back of the house, and
5 put a saucer of milk in front of its nose. We told Mother not to go near it while we were at school. When we came home from school, we crept quietly into the room, and there we saw the rabbit still sitting unmoving in the piece of cloth.

'Why won't it drink its milk, Mother?' we whispered. Our
10 father was still asleep.

'It prefers to die of loneliness. Silly little thing.'

We tried putting leaves to its nose. It sat like a stone. But its eyes were bright.

At dinner time, however, it had hopped a few inches, out of
15 the cloth, and there it sat again, a little brown lifeless mound. Only its side moved slightly with life.

Darkness came. My father went off to work. The rabbit was still sitting there unmoving. We began to feel desperate. Once more the rabbit was wrapped in the piece of old cloth. But now
20 it was carried into a dark corner of the spare room. We piled up an old blanket and tried to make it look like a rabbit's burrow, then put the rabbit inside. We put saucers of food and milk on the floor, so that if the little creature did come out and hop about, it would be sure to come upon some food. Then we
25 closed the door.

Next morning when it was light I went downstairs. Opening the door, I heard a slight sound. Then I saw little pools of milk all over the floor and tiny rabbit-droppings in the saucers. And there was the little creature, the tips of his ears showing behind
30 a pair of boots. He sat bright-eyed, twitching his nose and looking at me. He was alive, very much alive. But still we were afraid of frightening him.

'Don't go inside, Father. The rabbit's alive!'

'I'm sure he is,' said my father.
35 'Be careful how you go in.'

By evening, however, the little creature was tame, quite tame. We gave him the name Adolf. We were fascinated by him. We could not really love him, because he was wild but he was a delight. We decided he was too small to live in a cage outside. He must live in the house. My mother protested, but we won so we kept him upstairs, and when he dropped his tiny pills on the bed we laughed. 5

Rabbit games

Adolf instantly made himself at home. He had the house to himself, and he was perfectly happy, with his tunnels and his holes behind the furniture. We loved him to take meals with us. He would sit on the table with his back up, sipping his milk, shaking his whiskers and his little ears, hopping backwards and 10 forwards. He did not seem to care about anything. Then he would suddenly sit up and listen. He made his way over to the sugar-bowl, reached his tiny paws up to the edge of the bowl, and looked inside then tried to lift out a lump.

'I won't have this! Animals in the sugar-bowl!' cried my 15 mother, and banged her hand down on the table.

This gave Adolf such a fright that he kicked back his legs and knocked over a cup.

'It's your fault, Mother. If you would leave him alone.'

He continued to have his dinner with us. He rather liked 20 warm tea. And he loved sugar. Having eaten a lump, he would turn to the butter. But our parents would not allow that! He soon learned not to take any notice of Mother. Still, she hated him to put his nose in the food. And he loved to do it. One day between them they knocked over the milk-jug. Adolf jumped 25 back in horror, was seized by his little ears by my mother and dropped down onto the floor. He sat there for a moment not knowing what to do, and suddenly set off in a wild flight to the living-room.

That was his happy hunting ground. He had developed the 30 bad habit of chewing at the carpet. When chased away from this pasture he would run and hide under the sofa. There he would sit quietly — as if he were praying, until suddenly, no one knew why, he would run off and then we would hear him hurtling into the kitchen, but before we could follow, Adolf would flash past us, on an electric wind that swept him round the living-room again and carried him back, a mad little thing, flying like a ball round the house. And after it was over he would sit in a corner as if nothing had happened, his whiskers twitching.

Alas, he grew up rapidly. It was almost impossible to keep him from getting out of the front door.

One day, as we were playing outside, I saw his brown shadow make its way across the road and pass into the field that faces the houses. Instantly there was a cry of "Adolf!" A cry he knew very well. And instantly a wind sped him away down the sloping meadow, his tail bouncing through the grass. We ran after him. It was a strange sight to see him with his ears back leaving the world behind him. We ran until we were out of breath, but we could not catch him. Then somebody managed to run in front of him, and he sat without a worry, twitching his nose under a bush.

His wandering sometimes gave him a shock. One Sunday morning we heard a horrible scream from the yard. We rushed out. There sat Adolf crouching in terror under a bench, while a great black and white cat hissed at him, a few yards away. It was a strange sight.

How we hated that cat! We chased it over the back fence and across the neighbour's garden.

Adolf was still only half-grown but he was becoming too much for Mother. He dropped too many little pills all over the house. And to hear him bouncing down the stairs when she was alone in the house often gave her a fright. And to keep him inside was impossible. It was worse than having a child to look after.

But we would not keep him shut up inside a cage. He became stronger than ever. He was a strong kicker, and many times he gave us a scratch on the face or arms. He became wilder and wilder.

Mother's white curtains were the worst thing. She was very proud of them. They reached from the ceiling to the floor.

Adolf loved to get behind them and play, as if he were in the middle of a field of long grass. He had already torn several holes in them. One day he became completely caught up in them. He kicked and rolled around in a mad ball. He screamed and pulled and suddenly the curtain-rod, the curtains and all came down with a smash, right on top of one of my mother's favorite plants, just as she rushed in. She pulled him out from the mess, but she never forgave him. And he never forgave her either. A wicked wildness had come over him.

Adolf has to go

Even *we* understood that he must go. It was decided that my father should carry him back to the woods. Once again he was put inside the big pocket in Father's old jacket. And so, next day, our father said that Adolf, set down at the edge of the woods, hopped away, neither happy nor sad. We heard it and believed but inside we felt very unhappy. How would the other rabbits receive him? Would they smell that he was different, that he had lived with humans? Would they reject him? My mother laughed at the idea.

However, he was gone, and we were rather relieved. My father looked out for him. He said that several times as he was walking through the woods in the early morning, he had seen Adolf peeping from behind a clump of grass. He had called him, but Adolf had not responded. His animal's wildness had quickly taken him over again.

I myself would go to the edge of the woods and call softly. Sometimes I imagined I saw those bright eyes looking out from behind the bushes, the flash of a white tail. Was it Adolf?

8
The Blue Moccasins*

The fashion in women changes nowadays even faster than women's fashions. At twenty, Lina McLeod was thoroughly modern. At sixty, she was almost obsolete!

She started off in life to be almost independent. In those
5 days, forty years ago, when a woman said she was going to be independent, it meant she was not interested in men. She did not want to be dominated by a man. She would live her own life, manless.

Miss McLeod had an income from her mother. Therefore, at
10 the age of twenty, she escaped from the tyranny* of her father and went to Paris to study art. Then when she knew all about art, she travelled. Africa, China, the Rocky Mountains of Canada, and the deserts of Arizona. She knew them all. It was her way of showing her independence.
15 It was in New Mexico that she purchased the blue moccasins. They were covered with tiny blue beads. She bought them from an Indian guide.

Miss McLeod comes home
When the war broke out she came home. She was then forty-five, and her hair was already going grey. Her brother, two
20 years older than herself, but a bachelor, went off to the war; she stayed at home in the small family mansion in the country, and did what she could. She was small, stood very straight and never said very much when she spoke. Her face was like pale ivory, her skin, fine and tight, and her eyes were very blue. She
25 never wore make-up. Serious, with no nonsense about her, everyone in the town had a tremendous respect for her.

---

moccasins, shoes made of soft leather. *tyranny*, cruel use of authority.

In her various activities she often came into contact with Percy Barlow, the clerk at the bank. He was only twenty-two when she first saw him, in 1914, and she immediately liked him. He was a stranger in the town; the son of a country vicar in Yorkshire. But he was the sort of person who liked to confide 5 in people. He soon confided in Miss McLeod, whom he greatly respected. He told her all about his step-mother, whom he disliked, how he feared his father, and how he did not really have a home. It was almost tragic, but somehow, still a little amusing to Miss McLeod. 10

He was a good-looking boy, with stiff dark hair and odd, twinkling grey eyes under thick dark eyebrows, and a rather full mouth and a strange, deep voice. It was his voice that made Miss McLeod feel just a little uneasy. Barlow, on the other hand, regarded her with great respect. 'She's miles above 15 me,' he would say.

When she watched him playing tennis, letting himself go a bit too much, hitting too hard, running too fast, being too nice to his partner, she felt protective towards him. He was an orphan! Why should he go away to the war and be shot? She 20 found all sorts of things for him to do with her, all kinds of war-work. He was absolutely willing to do everything she wanted. He was devoted to her.

The marriage

But at last came the time when he had to go. He was now twenty-four and she was forty-seven. He came to say goodbye 25 in his awkward fashion. She suddenly turned away, leaned her head against the wall, and burst into bitter tears. He was frightened. Before he knew what was happening he had his arm in front of his face and was crying too.

She came to comfort him. 'Don't cry, dear, don't. It will be 30 all right.'

At last he wiped his face on his sleeve and looked at her shyly.

'It was your crying that I couldn't stand,' he said. Her blue eyes were brilliant with tears. She suddenly kissed his face.

'You are such a dear!' she said. Then she added, her tight white skin suddenly turning pink. 'It wouldn't be right for you to marry an old thing like me, would it?'

5 He looked at her in shocked silence.

'No, I'm too old,' she quickly added.

'Don't talk about old. You're not old,' he said. 'Not as far as I'm concerned. And if I thought you wanted me, I'd be proud if you married me. I would, I assure you.'

10 'Would you?' she said, still teasing him.

Nevertheless, the next time he was home on leave, she married him, very quietly, but very definitely. He was a young lieutenant. They stayed in her family home, Twybit Hall, for the honeymoon. It was her house now that her brother was

15 dead. And they had a strangely happy month.

Then he went off to Gallipoli and became a captain. He came home in 1919, sick with malaria, but otherwise in good health. She was in her fiftieth year, and she was almost white-haired; long, thick white hair, arranged perfectly, and with a

20 perfect, creamy, colourless face, with very blue eyes.

He was a little shocked to see her white hair. However he tried not to think about it, and loved her. And though she was frightened, she was happy. But she was bewildered. It always seemed awkward to her, that he would come wandering into

25 her room when she was brushing her hair. And he would sit there, silent, watching her brush the long silvery streams of hair, her arm working in a strange, mechanical motion. He would sit as if he were in a trance, just gazing. And she would at last glance round sharply, and he would rise, saying some

30 casual little thing to her and smiling at her oddly with his eyes. Then he would go out silently. And she would feel dazed, as if she did not quite know her own self any more.

They were alone in the house, except for the servants. He had no work. They lived modestly, for a good deal of her

35 money had been lost during the war. But she painted pictures. Marriage had stimulated her to this. She painted flowers, beautiful flowers that thrilled her soul. And he would sit

holding his pipe, silently watching her. He had nothing to do. He just sat and watched her small, neat figure as she painted. Then he emptied his pipe and filled it again.

She said that she was perfectly happy. And he said that he was perfectly happy. They were always together. He hardly ever went out, except to go riding. And practically nobody came to the house. 5

But still, they were very silent with one another. They did not seem to talk much any more. And he did not read much. He just sat still and smoked, and was silent. It annoyed her sometimes, and she would think as she had thought in the past, that the greatest happiness that one can experience is the happiness of being alone, quite, quite alone. 10

A new life

Then the bank he used to work for offered him a job as manager of the local branch, and she advised him to accept. Now he went out of the house every morning and came home every evening, which was much better. The minister of the local church asked him to sing in the church choir again, and again she advised him to accept. It was just like before he was married. He felt more like himself. 15 20

He was popular; a nice, harmless fellow, everyone said of him. Some of the men secretly pitied him. They took him home to lunch and introduced him to their families. He was popular with their daughters, for if ever they said they wanted something, he would say, 'What? Would you like it? I'll get it for you.' Or if it was something he could not do, 'I only wish I could do it for you.' And he meant it. 25

At the same time, although he was popular with the young ladies of the town, he was shy. He was without self-confidence, almost without a self at all. 30

The minister's daughter decided he needed to be woken up. And she was the one who was going to do it. She was exactly the same age as he was, a smallish, rather sharp-faced young woman who had lost her husband in the war. At first she had

thought it was a tragedy. Then she took the attitude of the young: you have got to live, so you may as well do it! She was a very kind woman, really. And she had a funny, little brown dog, a pomeranian, that she had bought in Italy in the street,
5 but which had turned out to grow quite handsome. Miss McLeod looked down on Alice Howells and her dog, so Mrs Howells felt no special love for Miss McLeod. That is what she used to call her. 'It's quite impossible to think of her as anything but old Miss McLeod!'
10 Percy was really more comfortable at the minister's house, where the dog barked all day and Mrs Howells changed her dresses three or four times a day, than he was in the deadly atmosphere of Twybit Hall, where Miss McLeod wore thick, long skirts and thick sweaters with her hair pulled up on top of
15 her head, and where she painted her wonderful pictures in the deepening silence of the daytime. At night she would change, after he came home. And though she liked to have him standing there as she did her hair, telling her something from the office, he worried her. When he was there, he could not
20 keep away from her. He would watch her, watch her, watch her, as if she were someone mysterious and from another world. Sometimes it made her angry. She was so used to her own privacy. What was he looking at? She never watched *him*. Rather she looked the other way. She was turning fifty.
25 He was quite happy playing tennis with Alice Howells and the rest. Alice was choir-mistress at the church. She was good at organizing people, though she was really a little unsure of herself. She was now over thirty, and had no one except her dog, her father, and the church. There was no one special in
30 her life. But she was cheerful, busy, and happy with her church and school-work, her dancing and her dressmaking.

She was fascinated by Percy Barlow. 'How can a man be so nice to *everybody?*' she asked him one day.

'Well, why not?' he replied, with the odd smile of his eyes.
35 'I don't mean that you shouldn't be, but how do you do it? How can you have so much good nature? I cannot be nice to everybody like you. You are always so kind.'

'Am I really?' he asked in a surprised voice.

He was like a man in a dream, or in a cloud. He was quite a good bank manager, in fact he was very intelligent. He was even quite good looking. He had plenty of brains, really. But his soul was asleep. And sometimes this made him look lifeless. 5 It made his body seem meaningless.

Alice Howells had always wanted to ask him about his wife. 'Do you love her?' she wanted to say. 'Can you really care for her?' But she did not dare ask him one word about his wife. Never. Not once. 10

Mrs Barlow, that is, Miss McLeod, stayed at home at Twybit Hall all the time. She did not even come in to church on Sunday. She never went to church any more. She watched her husband depart for church on Sunday, and felt a little resentful. He was going to sing in the choir! Yes, her marriage 15 was a humiliation* to her. She had married someone who was beneath her social class!

The years had gone by. She was now fifty-seven. Percy was thirty-four. He was still, in many ways, a boy. But in his curious silence, he was ageless. She managed him with perfect 20 ease. If she expressed a wish, he agreed at once. Their lives grew further apart. She twisted him round her little finger*. And yet secretly she was afraid of him. She wanted to be physically distant from him, which was why they had rooms at different ends of the house. He no longer seemed to care about 25 her. In some way, the mystery of her still fascinated him. But he did not love her. And secretly, she was rather glad.

It was in the late dark months of this year that she missed the blue moccasins. She had hung them on a nail in his room. Not that he ever wore them; they were too small. Nor did she; they 30 were too big. Moccasins are male footwear among the American Indians, not female footwear. But they were of a lovely deep-blue colour, made of little turquoise beads, with little flames of white and green. When, at the beginning of

*humiliation, something which makes a person humble. *twisted him round her little finger, could easily make him do anything she wanted.

77

their marriage he had admired them she had said, 'Yes, aren't they a lovely colour. So blue!'

And he had replied, 'Not as blue as your eyes though!'

So, naturally, she had hung them up on the wall in his room
5 and there they stayed. Till, one November day when there were no flowers, and she was trying to paint a picture with something blue in it. She wanted a special kind of blue. Turquoise blue. So she had gone to his room to look for the moccasins. And they were not there. Nor did the servants know
10 where they were.

So she asked him, 'Percy, do you know where those blue moccasins are, which hung in your room?' There was a moment's dead silence.

Then he looked at her with his twinkling eyes, and said, 'No,
15 I don't know anything about them.'

There was another silence. She did not believe him. But being a perfect lady, she only said as she turned away, 'Well, how curious it is!' And there was another silence. Then he asked what she wanted them for, and she told him. Then
20 nothing more was said.

A decision

It was November, and Percy was often out in the evenings now. He was rehearsing for a play which was to be given in the church schoolroom at Christmas. He had asked her about it. 'Don't you think it would be fun, for me to play one of the
25 characters?'

She looked at him trying to disguise her feeling of disgust: 'If *you* don't mind looking foolish,' she said.

'Oh, it doesn't upset *me* at all.'

'Then do it,' she said mildly.

30 How things have changed, she thought, when a bank manager, the husband of the owner of Twybit Hall, should take part in a theatrical performance on a schoolroom stage. She did not really want to know any more about it. She had a world of her own. It was a world of the past.

78

The play was to be performed for the first time, on Christmas Eve, and after the play, there was the midnight service in the church. So Percy told his wife not to expect him home until very late that night. He drove himself off in the car.

But as evening came, Miss McLeod began to feel a little *5* lonely. She was left out of everything. Life was slipping past her. It was Christmas Eve, and she was more alone than she had ever been. Percy only seemed to make her feel lonelier, leaving her like this.

She decided not to be left out. She would go to the play too. *10* It was already past six o'clock, and thinking about it had already made her feel quite irritated. It was raining and dark outside. Inside it was silent and lonely. She needed a car. She went to the telephone and rang up a garage in the nearby town. It was with great difficulty that she got them to promise *15* to send a car for her. Mr Slater would come for her himself in the two-seater.

She dressed nervously, in a dark-green dress with a few modest jewels. Looking at herself in the mirror, she still thought herself slim, young looking and distinguished. She did *20* not see how old-fashioned she was, with her long dress and her hair tied up the way she liked to wear it.

It was a three-mile drive in the rain, to the small country town. She sat next to Mr Slater, who was used to driving horses and was nervous and clumsy with a car. He drove without *25* saying a word and took her to the gate of St Barnabas's School. It was almost half past seven. The schoolroom was full of people. Everyone was very excited. 'I'm afraid we haven't a seat left, Mrs Barlow,' said a man who was standing at the door where people were still trying to get in. *30*

She looked at him with a determined look. 'Well, I shall have to wait somewhere, until Mr Barlow can drive me home,' she said. 'Couldn't you put me a chair somewhere?'

So the poor man went hurrying around trying to find a place for her. But the schoolroom was completely full. Then Mr *35* Simmons, the town's leading grocer, gave up his chair in the front row to Mrs Barlow, while he sat on a chair right under the stage where he could not see a thing. But he could see Mrs Barlow seated between his wife and daughter in the front row, speaking a word or two to them occasionally, and that was enough.

Two angry women

5   The lights went down. The play, *The Shoes of Shagput*, was about to begin. The curtains were drawn back, showing a little stage with a white cloth hanging at the back, painted to look like a middle-eastern palace. Then, in walked Percy, dressed as an Arab, with his face darkened. He looked quite handsome,
10   his grey eyes staring out of his dark face. But he was afraid of the audience. He spoke away from them, and moved around clumsily. Then after a certain amount of silly dialogue, the heroine came in. It was Alice Howells, of course. She was dressed in a white eastern robe, with a white veil over her face
15   and on her feet, the blue moccasins. The whole stage was white, except for the blue moccasins, Percy's dark-green belt, and a little boy's red cap.

When Mrs Barlow saw the blue moccasins, a little bomb of anger exploded in her. This, of all places! The blue moccasins
20   that she had bought in the deserts of Arizona. The blue moccasins that were not as blue as her own eyes! *Her* blue moccasins! On the feet of that creature, Mrs Howells!

Alice Howells was not afraid of the audience. She looked out confidently at them, lifting the veil over her eyes. And of
25   course she saw Mrs Barlow, sitting there like a judge, in the front row. And a bomb of anger exploded in her too.

In the play, Alice was the wife of a grey-bearded old lord, but a young man called Ali had fallen in love with her; Ali was played by Percy. The whole story of the play was the attempt of
30   these two to escape from the old master and his servants and get into each others' arms. The blue shoes were very important, because while the Sweet Leila wore them, Ali knew there was danger. But when she took them off, it meant that her husband was out and it was safe for him to approach her.

It was all quite childish, and everybody loved it, and Miss McLeod might have ignored the whole thing if it had not been for Alice Howells. Seeing Miss McLeod sitting there filled her mind with wicked thoughts. All these years she had been a poor widow, working for the church, trying to keep herself busy with all sorts of things so that she would not feel sorry for herself.

Now the sight of Miss McLeod sitting there in the front row, looking so calm and superior, filled her with courage and daring. A strange feeling came over her, and even her voice suddenly took on a different sound. She wanted to get even with Miss McLeod, sitting there so erect, with her great ball of white hair.

As Leila in the play, Alice was supposed to be sweet and tender with Percy. And so she was. Too, too sweet. In two minutes, she had him under a spell. He saw nothing of the audience. A faint, fascinated grin came over his face as he acted up to the young woman in the Arab dress. His voice changed and became clear, with a new sound to it. When the two sang together, it was with a most fascinating intimacy and affection. And when, at the end of Act One, the lovely Leila kicked off the blue moccasins, saying, 'Away, away, shoes of sorrow,' and danced a little dance alone, barefoot in front of her fascinated hero, his smile so enchanted that everyone else was enchanted and spellbound too.

Miss McLeod grew more and more angry. When the blue moccasins were kicked across the stage by Alice with the words "Away, away, shoes of sorrow," the elder woman grew pink with fury. She wanted to rise and snatch the moccasins from the stage and take them away. She sat in speechless rage during the brief interval between Act One and Act Two. Her moccasins! Her blue moccasins! Of the sacred blue colour. The blue of heaven!

The spell is broken

But there they were, in Act Two, on the feet of Alice. It was becoming too much. And the scenes between Alice and Percy were becoming more and more intense. Alice grew worse and worse.

5 She was worked up now, caught in her own spell, and unconscious of everything except Percy and the woman in the front row who owned him. Owned him? Ha-ha! For he was fascinated. The strange smile on his face, the look in his eyes, the way he leaned forward towards her, and the new sound to his voice: the audience had before them a man spellbound and
10 lost in passion.

Miss McLeod sat in shame and frustration, as if her chair was red-hot. She was outraged. The second act was working towards its climax. The climax came. The lovely Leila kicked off the blue shoes. 'Away, away, shoes of sorrow,' and she ran
15 barefoot to Ali, throwing herself in his arms. Percy looked as if he were in a dream, as he held her. While she, still aware of the audience and of Miss McLeod, looked at him with a look of triumph on her face.

Miss McLeod rose to her feet and looked towards the door.
20 But the way out was packed with people standing holding their breath as the two on the stage held each other in their arms. Miss McLeod could not bear it. She could not get out. She could not sit down again.

'Percy,' she said in a low, clear voice. 'Will you pass me my
25 moccasins?'

He lifted his face like a man wakened from a dream. He lifted his face from the face of Leila. His cold-grey eyes were like flames. He looked in horror at the white-haired woman standing below.
30 'What?' he said in a daze.

'Will you please hand me my moccasins?' she said, pointing to where they lay on the stage.

Alice had stepped away from him and was staring at the elderly woman at the front of the audience. Then she watched
35 him move across the stage, bend forward to pick up the blue moccasins, and stoop down to hand them over the edge of the stage to his wife, who reached up for them.

'Thank you,' said Miss McLeod, seating herself with the blue moccasins on her lap.

Alice recovered herself, gave a sign to the little orchestra, and began to sing at once, strong and assured, singing the part
5 that closed the act. She knew she could win the public to her side.

He too recovered at once, the little smile came back on his face and he calmly forgot his wife as he sang his part in the final song. Then it was finished. The curtains were pulled
10 across the stage. There was a loud cheering from the audience. The curtains opened, and Alice and Percy bowed to the audience, both smiling with their peculiar, secret smile, while Miss McLeod sat with the blue moccasins in her lap.

The curtains were closed. It was the interval between Act
15 Two and Act Three. After a few moments' hesitation, Mrs Barlow rose with dignity, and with the blue moccasins in her hand, moved towards the door. 'I would like to speak to Mr Barlow,' she said to the man who had shown her to her seat.

'Yes, Mrs Barlow.'

Percy is innocent

20 He led her round to a small room at the back where the actors and actresses were drinking lemonade and talking freely. Mrs Howells came forward and the man spoke to her. She turned to Percy.

'Percy, Mrs Barlow wants to speak to you. Shall I come with
25 you?'

'Oh. She wants to speak to me? All right.'

The two followed him to where Mrs Barlow stood, holding the moccasins. She was very pale, and she watched the two costumed figures approach as if they could not possibly be real.
30 She ignored Mrs Howells entirely.

'Percy,' she said. 'I want you to drive me home.'

'Drive you home?' he asked.

'Yes please.'

'Why? When?' he said, looking puzzled.

84

'Now, if you don't mind,' she said coldly.

'What? With me dressed up like this?' He looked at himself.

'I could wait while you change.'

There was a pause. He turned and looked at Alice Howells, and Alice Howells looked at him. The two women saw each other out of the corners of their eyes, but they refused to notice each other. He turned to his wife, his black face blank and his eyebrows raised.

'Well, you see,' he said, 'it's rather difficult right now. I can hardly ask them to keep Act Three waiting until I've taken you home and got back here again, can I?'

'So you want to play in the third act?' she asked coldly.

'Why, I must, mustn't I?' he said blankly.

'Do you wish to?' she said fiercely.

'Of course I do. I want to finish the thing properly,' he replied innocently.

She turned sharply away.

'Very well,' she said. And she called to the man who had shown her to her seat.

'Mr Jackson, will you please find a car to take me home.'

'Yes Mr Jackson,' called Percy, in his strong voice, going towards the man. 'Ask Tom Lomas if he will take my car and drive Mrs Barlow home. Thank you so very much.'

The three were left awkwardly alone again.

'I expect you have had enough with two acts,' said Percy soothingly to his wife. 'I know you don't enjoy these silly plays. They are childish. But, you see, they please the people. We have got a packed house, haven't we?'

His wife said nothing in answer. He looked so ridiculous, with his dark-brown face and his Arab clothes. And his mind was so completely innocent, as she knew when he turned to the other woman and said:

'We're just playing the fool, aren't we,' he said. His wife shivered.

'Absolutely,' said Alice, calmly.

She looked into his eyes, then she looked at the blue moccasins in the hand of the other woman. He gave a little jump, as if he had suddenly realized something for the first time.

At that moment Tom Lomas looked in, saying in a friendly manner:

5 'All right Percy. But I'll use my car. I feel more comfortable driving it than I do with yours.'

'Thanks very much. You're a great help.'

Then Percy turned to his wife and said in his most friendly and gentlemanly way:

10 'Would you mind leaving the blue moccasins for the next act? We will be in a bit of difficulty without them.'

'No I won't,' she said.

'What!' he exclaimed. 'Why? Why not? It's nothing but a play, to amuse the people. I can't see how it will hurt the

15 *moccasins*. I understand you don't like seeing me make a fool of myself. But anyhow, I'm a bit of a fool. I enjoy playing the fool, you know,' he said with a laugh. 'And after all, it doesn't really hurt *you* now, does it? Now, won't you leave us the moccasins for the last act.'

20 She looked at him, and then at the moccasins in her hand. No. She would not give up the moccasins. It was vulgar and common. She would be betraying herself and her standards.

'I'm sorry,' she said. 'But I really don't want them being used for this sort of thing. I never intended them to be.' She stood

25 with her face looking away from them.

He changed as if she had slapped his face. He sat down on top of a desk and stared around the room. Alice sat beside him in her white dress. They were like two sorry sparrows sitting on the branch of a tree. Miss McLeod walked towards the door.

30 'You'll have to think of something that will do instead,' he said to Alice, in a low voice. And leaning down he pointed to one of the grey shoes she had on.

Mr Lomas put his head through the door and muttered: 'The car's ready.'

35 'Oh good,' said Percy, with a forced cheerfulness. Then, making a great effort with himself, he stood up and went across to the door to his wife, saying to her in the same voice of false

86

cheer, 'You'll be fine with Tom. You won't mind if I don't come out? No, I'd better not show myself to the audience. Well, I'm glad you came, if only for a short time. Goodbye then. I'll be home late after the Christmas service at church. But I won't wake you when I get in. Goodbye. Don't get wet now.' And his voice, falsely cheerful, but stiff with anger, ended abruptly in silence.

Alice Howells sat silently. She was ignored. And she was unhappy, uneasy because of what had happened.

Love dies

Percy closed the door after his wife. Then he turned slowly to Alice and said, 'Just think of that now.'

She looked up at him anxiously. His face, was full of anger. His eyes blazed, and a great rush of rage seemed to be building up in him. For a second his eyes rested on her troubled, dark-blue eyes, then glanced away as if he did not want to look at her in his anger. Even so, she felt a touch of tenderness in his glance.

'And that's all she ever cared about; her own things and her own way,' he said in an angry whisper. Alice Howells hung her head in silence.

'No, nothing but herself,' his voice shook now with rage.

Alice Howells looked up at him in distress.

'Oh, don't say that!' she said. 'I'm sure she's fond of you.'

'*Fond* of me! Fond of *me*!' he shouted. 'It makes her sick to look at me. That woman has never been fond of anybody or anything, all her life. She couldn't be, that woman. She only cares about herself, and I've looked up to her as if she were a god. What a fool I am.'

Alice sat with her head dropped, realizing once more that men really are not fooled. She was upset, shaken by his rage, and frightened, as if she too were guilty. He sat down beside her. She glanced up at him.

'Never mind,' she said soothingly. 'You'll like her again tomorrow. You will feel differently about it tomorrow.'

87

THE THIMBLE AND OTHER STORIES

But he did not answer. Then after a while he added. 'She wouldn't even leave the moccasins. And she had hung them up in my room and left them there for years. They were as good as mine. And I did want this show tonight to be a success. What

5 are you going to do about it?'

'I've asked someone to get some blue slippers from my house. They'll do just as well,' she replied.

'Oh, really, it's too much.'

'You'll soon forget about it.'

10 'I don't know how I'm ever going to speak to her after that. I'm not going to go back home tonight.'

'Are you sure?' she asked.

He looked into her eyes. And in that look, he transferred his loyalty.

15 'You'll have to go on, Mrs Howells. We can't keep the audience waiting any longer.'

It was Jim Stokes, who was directing the show. They heard the clapping of the impatient audience.

'Goodness!' cried Alice Howells, hurrying to the door.

9
A Lesson on a Tortoise

It was the last lesson on Friday afternoon, and this, with Standard VI, was Nature Study from half past three till half past four. The last lesson of the week is tiring for both teacher and pupil. It is the end. There is no need to keep up the strictness and effort any longer, and finally the teacher gives in to fatigue. 5

Drawing Joey

But Nature Study is a pleasant lesson. I had got a big old tortoise, who had not yet gone to sleep, though it was in the middle of winter and the afternoons were dark. I knew the boys would still enjoy sketching him. I put him near the heater to 10 warm, while I went to get the shell of a dead tortoise that I had cut into two to show the bones under its shell. When I came back I found Joey, the old tortoise, slowly stretching his thin neck, and looking with two unmoving eyes at the two boys who were kneeling beside him. I was too tired to be angry with 15 them, too pleased with relief that it was Friday afternoon. So I told the class to get their Nature books out. I crouched down on my knees to look at Joey, and stroked his flat, dry head with my finger. He was quite lively. He spread out his legs and gripped the floor with his flat, hand-like paws, then he became 20 limp again as if he were about to drop off to sleep.

I felt pleased with myself, knowing that the boys would be delighted with the lesson. 'He won't want to walk,' I said to myself. 'And even if he is half asleep, they will be just as excited.' 25

There were about thirty boys in my class. It was a difficult, mixed class. Six were boys from a London boys' home, five boys came from a well-known home for the children of actors. Among the others were some who came to school in old shoes

that were falling apart, and others who came with a second
pair of soft, light shoes to wear inside on cold days.

    The Gordon boys were a difficult pair. They stood out from
the rest. Their hair was cut short, they wore rough clothes, and
5   did not trust anyone. They were very clever liars. The actors'
children were quite different. Some were gentle, and quite nice
looking. Others were polite, but did not really care about the
school.

    The boys crowded round the table noisily as soon as they
10   discovered Joey. 'Is he alive?' 'Look, his head is coming out.
He'll bite you.' 'He won't! Please sir, do tortoises bite?'

    I made them sit down and pulled the table up close to their
desks. Joey kept fairly still. The boys pushed against each other
excitedly, making comments about the poor reptile, looking
15   quickly from me to Joey and then to their neighbours. I told
them to begin drawing, but they were too excited to
concentrate.

    'Please sir, shall we draw the marks on the shell?'

    'Please sir, has he got only four toes?'
20   'Please sir, he's moving. Please sir!'

    I stroked his neck and calmed him down.

    'Now boys, don't make me wish I hadn't brought him out.
That's enough Miles. You will go back and draw leaves if I hear
you again. Enough now. Be still and get on with the drawing!'
25   I wanted peace for myself. They began to sketch diligently.

    I stood and looked across at the sunset which I could see
facing me through the window; a great sunset, very large and
magnificent, rising up in immense gold beauty beyond the
town that looked like a low dark strip of nothing under the
30   western sky. The light, the thick heavy golden sunlight, spread
on the desks and the floor like gold paint. I lifted my hands, to
let the sunlight fall on them, smiling faintly to myself.

The lesson is spoilt

    'Please sir.' I was suddenly interrupted. 'Please sir, can we
have some erasers?'

The question sounded rather hesitant. I had told the boys they were not allowed to have any more erasers. Someone had been stealing them from the cupboard and I was tired of trying to force them to tell me who it was. But it was Friday afternoon, very peaceful and happy. Like a bad teacher, I gave   5
in to them.

'All right then.'

My class monitor, a pale, bright boy, went to the cupboard and took out a red box.

'Please sir!' he cried, then he stopped and counted again in   10
the box.

'Eleven! There are only eleven, sir, and there were fifteen when I put them away on Wednesday.'

The class stopped, every face looking up. Joey sunk, and lay flat on his shell, his legs limp. It was another of those awful   15
moments. The sunset was blackened over in my mind. The charm of the afternoon was smashed like a glass that had fallen to the floor. My nerves seemed to tighten.

'Again.' I cried, turning to the class angrily, to the upturned faces, and the sixty watchful eyes.   20

'Again! I am sick of it, sick of it I am! You are nothing but thieves!' I was shaking with anger and distress.

'Who is it? You must know. You are all as bad as one another. You hide it!' I looked around the class for a guilty face. The Gordons, with their distrustful faces, were   25
noticeable.

'Marples,' I cried to one of them. 'Where are those erasers?'

'I don't know where they are. I have never seen them,' he almost shouted back at me, with an insolent tone to his voice. I was more angry.   30

'You must know! They have gone. They do not disappear by themselves. Who took them? Rawson? Do you know anything about them?'

'No sir!' he cried indignantly.

'No! You know nothing as usual. Gordon! What do you know   35
about these four erasers?'

'Nothing,' he shouted back angrily.

91

'Come here!' I cried. 'Come here! Bring me my stick, Burton. I am going to bring this thieving to an end!'

The boy dragged himself to the front of the class, and stood almost crouching, glaring at me. The rest of the boys sat
5 upright in their desks, like a pack of animals waiting to jump on me. There was total silence for a moment. Burton handed me my stick, and I turned from the class to Gordon.

'Now boy,' I said. 'You're going to get the stick for impertinence first.' He turned swiftly to me; there were tears in
10 his eyes.

Accusations

'Well,' he shouted at me. 'You always blame the Gordons. It's always us first.'

This was so untrue that it made me even angrier.

'That's not true.'

5 'Yes, you always start on us.'

'Well,' I answered, justifying myself. 'Isn't it natural? Haven't you boys stolen, several times, and been caught?'

'That doesn't mean we stole this time,' was the reply.

'How am I to know? You don't help me. How do I know?
10 Isn't it natural to suspect you?'

'Well, it's not us. We know who it is. Everyone knows who it is, only they won't tell.'

'Who knows?' I asked.

'Why, Rawson, and Maddock, and Newling, and all of
15 them.'

I asked these boys if they could tell me. Each one shook his head and said, 'No sir.' I went round the class. It was the same thing. They lied to me every one.

'You see,' I said to Gordon.

20 'Well, they don't want to tell you,' he said.

It was painful. I made them all sit down. I asked Gordon to write what he knew on a piece of paper, and I promised I would not tell the rest of the class. He refused. I asked the boys he had named. All of them refused. I asked them again. I
25 appealed to them.

'Let them all do it then,' said Gordon. I gave each boy a small piece of paper.

'Write on it the name of the boy you suspect. He is a thief and a sneak. He makes pain and trouble for all of us. It is your
30 duty.'

They wrote secretly and quickly folded up the papers. I collected them in the lid of the eraser box and sat at the table to examine them. There was dead silence, and they all watched me. Joey, the tortoise, had withdrawn into his shell,
35 forgotten. I envied Joey at that moment.

Knowledge without proof

A few papers were blank. Several had: I suspect nobody. I threw these in the waste-paper basket. Two had the name of an old thief. Eleven had the name of my assistant class monitor. He was a handsome boy, one of the oldest from the group of actors' children. I remembered how polite he had been when I 5
had asked him. I remembered the way his eyes shifted uneasily during the questioning. I remembered how eager he had been to do things for me before the monitor came into the room. I knew he was the one.

'Well,' I said, feeling very uncomfortable when I was 10
convinced the papers were right. 'Go on with the drawing.'

They were very uneasy and restless, but quiet. From time to time they watched me. Very shortly the bell rang. I told the two monitors to collect everything, and I sent the class home.

When the monitors had finished, and I had turned out all 15
the lights except one, I sent Curwen home, and kept my assistant monitor a moment.

'Segar, do you know anything about my erasers?'

'No sir.' He had a deep, manly voice, and he spoke confidently, but blushed. 20

'No? Nor my pencils, nor my two books?'

'No sir. I know nothing about the books!'

'No? The pencils then?'

'No sir. I don't know anything about them.'

'Nothing Segar?' 25

'No sir.'

He hung his head, and looked so ashamed and humiliated, a fine handsome lad, that I gave up. Yet I knew he would be dishonest again, when the opportunity arose.

'Very well! You will not help as monitor any more. You will 30
not come into the classroom until the class comes in. Do you understand?'

'Yes sir.' He was very quiet.

'Go along then.'

He went out, and silently closed the door. I turned out the 35
last light, shut the cupboards, and went home.

I felt very tired, and very sick. The night had come up, the clouds were moving darkly, and the streets near the school looked hateful in the lamplight.

Questions

1
The Thimble

A. What had first impressed the woman about her husband?
B. "The man himself was something different, something she was afraid of." Explain why the woman later felt like this about her husband.
C. Write a few sentences explaining the character of the woman.
D. What was the meaning of the thimble (a) for the woman and (b) for her husband?

2
Prelude

A. Describe how the boys dressed themselves for the play.
B. In this story Fred is proud. How do we know this? Explain how pride kept Fred and Nellie apart for so long.

3
A Shattered Dream

A. Describe the meeting between the youth and the story-teller.
B. With your partner, act out the conversation they had.
C. In your opinion, who was Muriel?
D. Imagine that you discover an intruder in your home. Write an account of what happens and what is said.

97

4
Lessford's Rabbits

A. Why did Lessford take extra pieces of bread at breakfast?
B. Some of the children came from poor homes. Find evidence in the story to support this statement.

5
Rex

A. Why did the children's mother pretend to hate the dog?
B. How did a) the children b) the mother c) the father and d) the uncle treat Rex?
C. If you had a dog how would you treat it?

6
The Princess

A. Why did the girl's father always refer to her as "the Princess"?
B. "Her father let her see the world from the outside." Explain.
C. How did the Princess feel after Romero's death?

7
Adolf

A. Why had it proved impossible to tame the rabbit?
B. Give the arguments for and against keeping a rabbit as a pet.

98

8
The Blue Moccasins

A. Explain the importance of the blue moccasins in the Christmas play and in the story. Was there a connection between the two? Explain.
B. Does your sympathy lie with Miss McLeod (Mrs Barlow) or with her husband Percy? Give reasons for your answer.
C. Why do you think Alice tried to torment Mrs Barlow?

9
A Lesson on a Tortoise

A. Why were the children drawing the tortoise?
B. How did the teacher find who had stolen the erasers?
C. Explain how the teacher felt at the beginning of the lesson and how he felt at the end.

Oxford Progressive English Readers

Introductory Grade

Vocabulary restricted to 1400 headwords
Illustrated in full colour

The Call of the Wild and Other Stories	Jack London
Emma	Jane Austen
Jungle Book Stories	Rudyard Kipling
Life Without Katy and Seven Other Stories	O. Henry
Little Women	Louisa M. Alcott
The Lost Umbrella of Kim Chu	Eleanor Estes
Stories from Vanity Fair	W.M. Thackeray
Tales from the Arabian Nights	Retold by Rosemary Border
Treasure Island	R.L. Stevenson

Grade 1

Vocabulary restricted to 2100 headwords
Illustrated in full colour

The Adventures of Sherlock Holmes	Sir Arthur Conan Doyle
Alice's Adventures in Wonderland	Lewis Carroll
A Christmas Carol	Charles Dickens
The Dagger and Wings and Other Father Brown Stories	G.K. Chesterton
The Flying Heads and Other Strange Stories	Retold by C. Nancarrow
The Golden Touch and Other Stories	Retold by R. Border
Great Expectations	Charles Dickens
Gulliver's Travels	Jonathan Swift
Hijacked!	J.M. Marks
Jane Eyre	Charlotte Brontë
Lord Jim	Joseph Conrad
Oliver Twist	Charles Dickens
The Stone Junk	Retold by D.H. Howe
Stories of Shakespeare's Plays 1	Retold by N. Kates
Tales from Tolstoy	Retold by R.D. Binfield
The Talking Tree and Other Stories	David McRobbie
The Treasure of the Sierra Madre	B. Traven
True Grit	Charles Portis

Grade 2

Vocabulary restricted to 3100 headwords
Illustrated in colour

The Adventures of Tom Sawyer	Mark Twain
Alice's Adventures Through the Looking Glass	Lewis Carroll
Around the World in Eighty Days	Jules Verne
Border Kidnap	J.M. Marks
David Copperfield	Charles Dickens
Five Tales	Oscar Wilde
Fog and Other Stories	Bill Lowe
Further Adventures of Sherlock Holmes	Sir Arthur Conan Doyle

Grade 2 (cont.)

The Hound of the Baskervilles	Sir Arthur Conan Doyle
The Missing Scientist	S.F. Stevens
The Red Badge of Courage	Stephen Crane
Robinson Crusoe	Daniel Defoe
Seven Chinese Stories	T.J. Sheridan
Stories of Shakespeare's Plays 2	Retold by Wyatt & Fullerton
A Tale of Two Cities	Charles Dickens
Tales of Crime and Detection	Retold by G.F. Wear
Two Boxes of Gold and Other Stories	Charles Dickens

Gade 3

Vocabulary restricted to 3700 headwords
Illustrated in colour

Battle of Wits at Crimson Cliff	Retold by Benjamin Chia
Dr Jekyll and Mr Hyde and Other Stories	R.L. Stevenson
From Russia, with Love	Ian Fleming
The Gifts and Other Stories	O. Henry & Others
The Good Earth	Pearl S. Buck
Journey to the Centre of the Earth	Jules Verne
Kidnapped	R.L. Stevenson
King Solomon's Mines	H. Rider Haggard
Lady Precious Stream	S.I. Hsiung
The Light of Day	Eric Ambler
Moonraker	Ian Fleming
The Moonstone	Wilkie Collins
A Night of Terror and Other Strange Tales	Guy De Maupassant
Seven Stories	H.G. Wells
Stories of Shakespeare's Plays 3	Retold by H.G. Wyatt
Tales of Mystery and Imagination	Edgar Allan Poe
20,000 Leagues Under the Sea	Jules Verne
The War of the Worlds	H.G. Wells
The Woman in White	Wilkie Collins
Wuthering Heights	Emily Brontë
You Only Live Twice	Ian Fleming

Grade 4

Vocabulary within a 5000 headwords range
Illustrated in black and white

The Diamond as Big as the Ritz and Other Stories	F. Scott Fitzgerald
Dragon Seed	Pearl S. Buck
Frankenstein	Mary Shelley
The Mayor of Casterbridge	Thomas Hardy
Pride and Prejudice	Jane Austen
The Stalled Ox and Other Stories	Saki
The Thimble and Other Stories	D.H. Lawrence